GiftAid Donation

CW00404955

Prayer Flags

The Life and Spiritual Teachings of Jigten Sumgön

Prayer Flags

The Life and Spiritual Teachings of Jigten Sumgön

Translated by
KHENPO RINPOCHE KÖNCHOG GYALTSEN

Snow Lion Publications
Ithaca, New York USA

Snow Lion Publications
P.O. Box 6483
Ithaca, New York 14851
USA

Copyright © 1984, 1986

First Edition U.S.A. 1984 Khenpo Rinpoche Könchog
Gyaltsen
Second Edition U.S.A. 1986 Khenpo Rinpoche Könchog
Gyaltsen

All rights reserved. No part of this book may be reproduced
by any means without prior written permission from the
publisher.

Library of Congress Catalogue Number 86-22070

ISBN 0-937938-37-8

Library of Congress Cataloging-in-Publication Data

'Bri-gun Chos-rje 'Jig-rten-mgon-po, 1143-1217.
Prayer flags.

Translated from Tibetan.

1. 'Bri-gun-pa (Sect) — Doctrines. 2. Spiritual life (Buddhism) 3.
Mahāmudrā (Tantric rite)
I. Gyaltsen, Khenpo Rinpochay Könchok, 1946-
II. Title.
BQ7684.4.N742   1986   294.3'923   86-22070
ISBN 0-937938-37-8

Contents

Foreword

Because of the profoundly religious character of Tibetan society, virtually all Tibetan literature must be considered religious in nature. The majority of Tibetan literature consists of translations of Sanskrit Buddhist works of Indian origin. The emphasis on accuracy which these translations demanded left little allowance for a Tibetan literary style. There are, however, three distinct literary forms which have developed along uniquely Tibetan lines. These are the religious biography, the extemporaneous spiritual song, and what might best be described as guides to various aspects of the spiritual path sometimes called "religious discourses". This small publication offers a brief introduction to all three of these distinctly Tibetan literary forms.

Tibetan biography is the most stylized of the three and may give the new reader somewhat of a start. One is suddenly transported to a world where stones turn into frogs and men leave footprints on solid rock. Without commenting on the veracity of such events, one can easily see the symbolism when the teacher expands the size of his cave by lifting the ceiling. Likewise, the moral of a stolen jewel that turns into a frog is readily apparent. In Western literary tradition, stylized forms are often used to introduce mythic literature.

"Once upon a time" is the classic stylized cue which tells us to open the door to fantasy and judge not with the ordinary mind but appreciate and experience the subconscious symbolism of the tale. Likewise, the Tibetan religious biography is filled with cues that function to place the devout reader in a specific state of mind. Lest such a psychological interpretation be a little too facile, it should be pointed out that the root nature of Tibetan literature is the study of "mind" and its relation to what we call reality. Likewise, these seemingly fantastic occurrences described in Tibetan biographies continue to be reported up into the present day even by unbiased and educated Western observers.

If the function of the biography is to place the reader in an exalted state of fantasy, the spiritual song is its antithesis. The spiritual song cuts through the soft flesh of illusion to the bone of reality. The imagery here is quite appropriate; there is a certain starkness to the form with ample use of paradox to cut away preconceived ideas of reality. At their best, such songs provide the reader with an often abrupt "pointing out" of the real nature of the human condition — a condition which, when exposed with clarity, cannot be hidden by the flights of intellectual fantasy.

The final form, the religious philosophical discourse, will undoubtedly be the most comfortable for the Western reader. Though usually more condensed than its Western counterpart, the similarity to Western philosophical writing from Plato to Sartre will be readily apparent. The short description of the path of Mahamudra is the clearest exposition I have seen of this profound tantric teaching. These three short pieces come to us like a timeless breeze. For this we owe a great debt of gratitude to Khenpo Könchog Rinpoche and his students.

D.A. Shanelec
Santa Barbara, California
July 1984

Introduction

To dispel all suffering and the causes of suffering, and to establish all beings in the ultimate state of peace and happiness, Lord Buddha gave the limitless teachings of sutra and tantra. Thus, he benefited sentient beings. Later, in the northern Land of Snow, he took birth again as the peerless Kyöbpa Jigten Sumgyi Gönpo, the Great Drikungpa, Ratna Shri. With his immeasurable compassionate wisdom, he turned the vast Wheel of Dharma for limitless sentient beings.

The Kagyudpa lineage was founded in India by the great yogi Tilopa (988-1069) and was brought to Tibet by Marpa (1012-1096), the great translator and the principle disciple of Naropa (1016-1100). Marpa translated many important works of both sutra and tantra of the Lord Buddha. The principle disciple of Marpa was Milarepa (1052-1135), who attained enlightenment in one lifetime and became a key inspiration for dharma practitioners. Milarepa's chief disciple was Gampopa (1079-1153) whose coming was prophesied clearly by the Lord Buddha. Gampopa gathered many disciples and through them the the Buddha's teachings flourished like the rising sun. From Gampopa there came the four elder lineages which are: Barom Kagyu,

Tselpa Kagyu, Kamtshang or Karma Kagyu, and Phagdru Kagyu. Gampopa composed the *Jewel Ornament of Liberation, The Precious Garland of the Excellent Path,* and other works. His principle disciple was Phagdru Dorje Gyalpo (1110-1170) who gathered together 80,000 disciples and thus benefited many sentient beings. From Phagdru Dorje Gyalpo came the eight younger Kagyudpa schools which are: Drikung Kagyu, Taklung Kagyu, Drukpa Kagyu, Trophu Kagyu, Yelpa Kagyu, Martsang Kagyu, and Yasang Kagyu. Jigten Sumgön (1143-1217) was the successor of Phagdru Dorje Gyalpo and because of this the Drikung Kagyu school is considered both an elder and a younger school.

There was no other great teacher in Tibet who gathered together so many disciples as Jigten Sumgön. The great Jamgön Köngtrul Rinpoche said in his *Knowledge Treasure Text (She-ja Dzo):*

The mountains are filled with Drikungpa
    practitioners,
and all the plains are filled with Drikungpa patrons.

Many of Lord Jigten Sumgön's disciples attained enlightenment in one lifetime. He was the father of all Kagyudpas; many great teachers of his time came to him expressing great devotion and faith and thus received many teachings.

From Jigten Sumgön until the present time there has been a continuous line of highly realized Drikung yogis. The most famous of these express the qualities of the sun and moon.

The main study and practice of the Drikung Kagyudpa are the *Fivefold Profound Path of Mahamudra* and *The Six Yogas of Naropa,* the most profound philosophy text, the *Gong Chig,* which has numerous commentaries by many great scholars, the *Essence of Mahayana Teaching (Thegchen Tanpa'i Nyingpo), The Stages and the Path of Both Sutra and Tantra Form,* and many other profound teachings from Lord Jigten Sumgön.

In the *Fivefold Profound Path* are included all the teachings of Lord Buddha. These five paths are: 1) the practice of bodhicitta; 2) yidam practice; 3) the guru yoga four kayas practice; 4) Mahamudra practice; 5) dedication of sharing merit practice. If any of these practices are missing, then the fruit will not ripen. Here in this book is a very brief translation of an explanation of the practice itself. There are many other texts which describe the *Fivefold Profound Path* in much more detail.

These days, in the West, many people are interested in the Buddha's teachings. To kindle the flame of their understanding, I have translated — with the kind help of Richard Finney — a short life-story of Jigten Sumgön and some of his vajra songs. It is like taking a drop of water from the ocean. With the kind help of Ani Tsering Cho'dron, the *Fivefold Profound Path* was translated.

By virtue of this work, may all sentient beings open the eye of wisdom, enjoy temporary peace and happiness, and ultimately attain enlightenment.

The Life of Gampopa

The milk-like ocean of view-meditation-action
Is churned into the butter of enlightened wisdom.
I bow to the peerless Gampopa who caused
The teachings of the Buddha to flourish and
United the lineage of the Kadampa and
Mahamudra.

Gampopa, the principal disciple among all the disciples of Milarepa, is like a sun among stars. As Marpa said in explaining Milarepa's dream of the four pillars wherein "a vulture had a chick that will be the Peerless One," this refered to a great disciple, Gampopa Dzamling Drakpa[1], who would come to Milarepa from the north. Milarepa also had a dream wherein it was prophesied that Gampopa would come. In the dream Gampopa came to him carrying an empty crystal vase which Milarepa filled with nectar from his silver vase. Moreover, Buddha himself had predicted his coming.

Before the time of Buddha Shakyamuni, Gampopa had been born as the dharma teacher Metok Dazeh. During the time of Buddha Shakyamuni, he was born as Chandraprabhava.

In order to spread the Practice Lineage in Tibet, he was born in the Water Tiger Year at Sewa Lung in Nyel in Central Tibet. His father's name was Nyiwa Gyalpo, his mother's Ngalsa. He had three brothers. He was married for twelve years and had a son and a daughter. It happened that, during a wide-spread epidemic, his two children died and his wife also became ill. As she lay dying she confessed to him, "I am dying, and when I am dead you will marry a beautiful woman [and forget me]." He promised instead that he would become a monk. Her heart at ease, she died.

Gampopa was greatly saddened by these losses and true to his promise he became a monk under the spiritual teacher Shawa Ling and was named Sonam Rinchen. From this teacher and the great Cha-dul[2] he got the teaching of the Six Treatises of the Kadampa[3] and other teachings, and mastered them. He received the Chakrasamvara empowerment and meditation instruction from Loden Sherab of Mongyul[4]. From the spiritual teachers Chayulwa, Chakri-kongkawa, and Nyukrumpa, he studied all the teachings of Jowa Atisha[5]. Thus his understanding of the Buddha's teaching was fully developed.

He lived in a magnificient mansion and practiced meditation there with one-pointed mind. He received signs, both in dreams and while awake, that he had attained the tenth level of the bodhisattva[6], as described in the *Suvarnaprabhasa Sutra*.

Once, in the spring, he went for a walk outside the grounds of his mansion. He chanced upon three beggars and from one of them heard the name of Milarepa. When he heard this name his mind became completely enraptured and tears of devotion burst forth.

He was like a passionate youngster seeing a beautiful goddess or like the sudden rustling of the leaves of an apple tree agitated by the wind. He was confused about what to do next. He returned home and tried to do his main practice — the seven-branched prayer[7] — but was unable to do so. He couldn't understand it and wondered what was happening to his mind.

Before going to sleep, he practiced a profound meditation, achieved the state of one-pointedness, and recognized that all phenomena were void. He could also read the minds of all sentient beings. Arising from that meditation, he went searching for the three beggars. He found them sleeping in an inn and asked them where Milarepa was, who his teacher was, what teachings he gave, and what special qualities he had.

The eldest of the beggars replied, "He stays in Gungthang and his master was Marpa the Translator, the disciple of the great pandita Naropa. He teaches the Six Yogas of Naropa[8] from the *Hevajra Tantra*. Many people come to see him but each sees him differently. I myself, however, have not seen him." Gampopa then offered them much food and hospitality.

That night he went to sleep praying one-pointedly to Milarepa. In a dream he blew a great trumpet — there was none larger in Central Tibet. It sound pervaded the entire universe. He then beat a huge gong. Next, a woman gave him a large drum and asked him to beat it for mankind. She then gave him a skull-cup filled with milk and asked him to offer it to all animals. She told him to drink of it when he was thirsty and that his drinking would quench the thirst of all beings of the six realms. Then she said, "I will now go to the north." Thus he dreamed[9].

When he awoke in the morning, he decided to go to Milarepa. He sold his house and land, collected sixteen ounces of gold and some tea, and then went to say good-bye to his old teachers. Disappointed, they said, "We beat the big copper gong but another will make the sound. It is inevitable. Even dog fat is acceptable if it heals the wound. Do not give up our monastic traditions." Thus getting their permission, he went to see Milarepa.

When he arrived at a village near Trashigang where Milarepa was staying, Gampopa asked an old woman for information about Milarepa. She replied, "Yesterday I went to see Milarepa. He said, 'A son will come from

Central Tibet; whoever introduces him to me will not be reborn in the lower realms.' Therefore, my daughter will introduce you to Milarepa." Hearing this, Gampopa thought to himself, I must be a proper vessel indeed! Thus did his pride grow. Milarepa perceived this and refused to meet him for half a month. Instead, Sebanrepa[10] received him in a cave and requested that he wait there. After fifteen days, Milarepa received him at Trode Trashigang. Gampopa offered him the gold and tea. Milarepa responded, "Gold and this old man do not agree and I have no pot in which to boil tea." So he gave them back and told Gampopa to use them for his practice. Milarepa then asked, "What is your name?" "My name is Sönam Rinchen," Gampopa replied. Milarepa then repeated "Sönam" (Virtue) three times, and continued, "Virtue is accumulated by great accomplishments. You are indeed precious *(Rinchen)* to all sentient beings." Milarepa then gave Gampopa some nectar [containing alcohol] in a skull-cup. Gampopa had some doubts about this for he was still a monk [and thus forbidden alcohol]. Milarepa said, "Don't think so much! Just enjoy it!" Then Gampopa drank it all without hesitation. Milarepa understood by this that Gampopa was to hold the lineage of all the teachings. Milarepa then sang a Song of Reception.[11]

They then went to Chuwar in Manlung. Milarepa asked, "What empowerments and teachings do you have?" Gampopa explained in detail what he had received. Milarepa said, "Those are excellent and profound teachings which you received. I will also give you my lineage blessing." He then gave Gampopa the Sindura Mandala Vajrayogini empowerment and blessing.

At one point Gampopa proudly said, "I can remain seated in meditation for seven days." Milarepa just laughed and said, "You can't get oil by squeezing sand; you get oil by squeezing mustard seed. Practice my short AH Chandali yoga." Milarepa then gave him instructions in this practice. Gampopa meditated day and night and soon experienced the ten signs of success: smoke, etc. In dreams and other experiences he received signs that he had achieved the eight good qualities. All this he related to Milarepa in a song. Milarepa replied to him in a song which prophesied Gampopa's future, wherein he would benefit limitless sentient beings. He then said, "Cut off all attachment, whether in dreams or when awake. Keep all of this in your mind and see if it comes true or not. Then a true inner devotion to this old man will be born in you and you will realize the suchness of your mind."

Gampopa then practiced diligently. He saw the seven Medicine Buddhas[12] and other deities and the limitless Sambhogakaya buddha-field. He saw especially Rahula[13] — the size of a horse hair, yet eclipsing the sun and the moon. He repeated all this to Milarepa who said, "*Now* you are beginning to show promise! Now! Now you must go to Central Tibet and practice there. You will walk the dangerous path of psychic power. You must be careful with that. Mount Gampo Dar will be the place where you meditate and gather disciples."

As Gampopa was leaving for Central Tibet, Milarepa accompanied him for part of the way and sang a song of instruction to him.[14] Milarepa then gave him much special advice and renamed him Gelong Dorje Dzinpa Jamlung Trakpa (Bhikshu Vajra Holder Universally Renowned).

Before they parted Milarepa said, "I have a profound teaching for you." He led Gampopa behind a large nearby rock. He then raised the back of his robes and showed Gampopa his buttocks — all hard and calloused like a monkey's. "You have to keep sitting on one seat like this. Don't mention this to the others." He then said, "In the Rabbit Year on the fourteenth day of the first month, try to come to Drin and Nyanam."[15] Then the father and son parted.

Gampopa journeyed to Central Tibet and meditated in Oelkha and Nyel. After a while he remembered his master's instruction to return to Drin but the time had already passed. Nevertheless, he set off and when he had gotten as far as the Yarlung Valley he received word that Milarepa had entered into *parinirvana*. The messenger then gave him Milarepa's robe and staff. Gampopa was overcome by this news and fainted. When he came to he sang a song asking to meet Milarepa face to face once more. Then he sprinkled eight ounces of gold dust toward Nyanam and returned to Nyel. There he met a beautiful and wealthy young female incarnation who promised to sponsor his meditation practice.

Thus he stayed for six years at Sewalung in Nyel and for twelve years at Gelung in Oelkha. In those places he meditated continuously like a flowing river. He came to realize that all of samsara and nirvana are but dreams and illusions. In this way he came to attain the wisdom free from elaboration.

As Milarepa had predicted, Gampopa went to Daklha Gampo and built a meditation center, gathering many disciples from Central and Eastern Tibet like geese flocking to a lotus lake. There he gave vast and profound teachings according to the individual dispositions of the disciples. In this way the unified stream of the Kadampa and Mahamudra teachings dawned like the rising sun.

Gampopa was able to instantly manifest in many forms. When he gave a blessing he manifested as Shakyamuni Buddha. At other times he showed himself as the Great Compassionate One (Chenrezig) and many other yidams, buddhas, and bodhisattvas. He could hang his dharma robes on a sunbeam. When he meditated on one of the five elements he would seem to be like that element. He could sit on his monk's meditation cloth and float across a river and back. He could suspend his begging bowl in mid air. Thus he displayed many miracle powers and gave many teachings.

At the end of his life he said, "I have labored greatly for the Buddha's teaching and kindled the flame of wisdom in sentient beings who were so blind. Thus the work which was to be done for these disciples in this life has been done and for the sake of future generations I have composed many meaningful texts. I want to assure my disciples, now and to come, that if they rely on me I will protect them from the sufferings of samsara and birth in the lower realms. Therefore do not be sad."

This unsurpassable great master Gampopa dissolved the mandala of his manifested form on the fifteenth day of the sixth month of the Water Bird Year (1153 C.E.). At that time many wonders and miraculous signs, such as rainbows and celestial singing and rains of flowers, attracted many beings. When his physical form was cremated the tongue and heart would not burn. Many relics appeared in the ashes to be used for accumulating merit for sentient beings. The relics are even now [early 17th century] proliferating.

For all sentient beings who were connected with him, even if they were sinful, rainbows appeared and flowers rained when they died. By the power of his great compassion all those who were connected with him entered onto the path of enlightenment.

Notes

1. The full story may be found in Evans-Wentz: *Tibet's Great Yogi, Milarepa,* 149-155.
2. Chadul: A spiritual master of Kadampa.
3. The six treatises of the Kadampa are six Mahayana texts especially revered by the Kadampas. They are: *Buddhajataka; Dharmapada; Bodhicharyavatara; Shiksasamucya; Bodhisattvabhumi; Shravakabhumi.*
4. Loden Sherab: A spiritual master of Kadampa.
5. Atisha was a noted Indian teacher who came to Tibet and founded the Kadampa lineage.
6. The tenth level of the bodhisattva is the highest stage in a bodhisattva's development.
7. The seven-branched prayer: This is a simple ritual prayer that is capable of being elaborated into a full and complete meditation practice.
8. The Six Yogas: Chandali; Clear Light; Dream; Illusory Body; Bardo; Phowa.
These are advanced meditations employed in the higher yoga tantra practices.
9. Gampopa's dream is explained in the *Hundred Thousand Songs of Milarepa.*
10. Sebanrepa: One of Milarepa's close disciples.

11. See Chang, *Hundred Thousand Songs of Milarepa*, Vol. 2, p. 474.

12. The seven Medicine Buddhas: Bhaisjyaguru, Abhijnaraja, Dharmakirtisagaraghosa, Ashokottamashri, Suvarnabhadravimalarathaprbhasa, Ratnasshikhin, Suparikirtitanamashri.

13. Rahula eclipses the sun and moon.

14. See Chang: vol. 2, p. 494-5.

15. Milarepa was predicting the exact date of his death.

The Life of Phagmo Drupa

From the snow mountain of Buddha Khorwa Jig's
  enlightened attitude
An unbroken stream of compassion flows
  constantly and
Nurtures the growth of the Vajrayana garden.
May the Vajra King brighten the light of the heart
  essence of the dharma.

The principal disciple of the peerless Gampopa was Dro-gun Phagmo Drupa, the indisputable incarnation of Bud-dha Khorwa Jig. He was born into a poor family in the Iron Tiger Year (1111 C.E.) at Drilung Mesho in the Meh valley of Eastern Tibet. His father's name was Beh Adar. In an earlier incarnation he had been a forest monkey and had killed a dangerous poisonous snake. Due to the karma generated by that act, he was plagued all his life by a recurring pain in his shoulder.

As an infant he was able to remember many previous births, but when he was three years old his parents gave him some defiled meat and he lost that ability (although he regained it after completing his training under Gampopa). When he was nine his parents died and he became a novice monk under Abbot Tsultrim Bar. At that time he was given the name Dorje Gyalpo. He studied reading, writing, and icon painting. He also became physically very powerful like Tshempoche Drima Mepa.[1] For the next thirteen years he served sixteen different gurus and studied the sutras and tantras under them. When he was twenty-two, he journeyed to Central Tibet with his companion Beh Dorje. Along the way he met Acala and many other deities. Eventually he came to Sangphu Monastery where he studied and mastered the Prajnaparamita, logic, and Madhyamika under Tolung Gyamarwa and others. While there, he fell under the influence of some bad friends and helped to steal a yak. A spiritual teacher, one Chapa, set out to catch the thieves and show them the way to right conduct. His influence motivated Phagmo Drupa to practice contrition and purification for many years.

When Phagmo Drupa was twenty-five years old he became a fully ordained monk under Abbot Cha Duldzin, Tolung Gyamarwa, and Adar. Under these teachers he studied the extensive *vinaya* teachings.[2] The fame of his expertise in these matters spread widely. Not being satisfied with these teachings, he took from Chayulpa the Six Texts of the Kadampas[3] and other teachings. From Mar Chökyi Gyalpo he received the text of the Root Tantra of Chakrasamvara of the Naropa lineage. Then, with the great Galopa[4] he studied the Five-Deity Form of Chakrasamvara[5] and the Four-Armed Mahakala together with their mandalas, meditations, and instructions. Under Kunga Nyingpo, Bugom, Jomo Lharje, and many others he studied the Lam Dre teachings extensively.[6] He also received many tantra teachings and techniques from Changsem Dawa Gyaltsen, Nyanggom Sangye, and Nyil Chung. From Ngamsho Rinag he received a special prediction to the effect that he would benefit many sentient beings.

Hearing the fame of Gampopa, he went to meet him at Daklha Gampo. To that embodiment of all buddhas, the second omniscient one, the unsurpassable Dagpo Lharje, he bowed low. Offering a mandala with strong devotion and a stream of tears, an extraordinary faith was born in Phagmo Drupa's mind. He then told Gampopa of his life and meditation experience. Gampopa said, "You seem to think yours is a great attainment." Then holding out a handful of grain, he continued, "This is greater!" At that, Phagmo Drupa's previous *shamatha*[7] attainment vanished. Gampopa then said, "Sit on that rock and concentrate on your mind without creating a form." Phagmo Drupa did so and thus actualized the meaning of the Mahamudra.[8] At that instant a rainbow appeared, bridging the space between them, and Phagmo Drupa realized without error all of the Buddha's teachings. He then remained at Daklha Gampo, where he became known as one of the Three Men From Kham (along with Düsum Khyenpa — the first Karmapa — and Gompa Shawaton). These three demonstrated many miraculous powers such as raising the dead.

After Gampopa died, Phagmo Drupa remained in Daklha Gampo for a year and officiated at the cremation and last rites for Gampopa. As that master had predicted, Phagmo Drupa went to "All Good" Forest and established the famous "Glorious Phagdru" Monastery under the patronage of the king of Drak Khawa. His religious activities increased beyond limit. He gathered around him more than 80,000 disciples, among whom 500 attained the degree of liberation known as "Holding the Golden Umbrella."[9] From him descended the eight Kagyu orders: Drikung, Taklung, Lingre (Drukpa), Yemsang, Trophu, Marsang, Yelpa, and Shuksep. He became the head of all the streams of the Kagyu.

Once when the great spiritual teacher Shen Trongpa visited him, Phagmo Drupa had hung three paintings in his room: in the center Phadampa Sangye,[10] on the right the peerless precious master Dhagpo Lharje (Gampopa), and on the left Sachen Kunga Nyingpo. Shen asked him why they were arranged so. He answered that Phadampa Sangye had been his teacher for many lifetimes, especially at the Temple of Tsip in Nyangto where he received the Zhi Jed teaching[11] and many others. Likewise, the Lords Gampopa and Sachen had been his teachers for many lifetimes. Moreover, the Lord of All Beings (Phagmo Drupa) received visionary teachings from the great Brahmin Saraha, Arya Asanga, Shantideva, Chandrakirti, and many other great mahasiddhas as well as Vajrayogini and many other yidams. Thus, people who have strong devotion and faith can see him in the form of the Buddha Shakyamuni, Avalokiteshvara, Chakrasamvara, and others [according to their level of mental development].

From age forty-nine until he died at age sixty-one his daily schedule was: during the waxing moon he did solitary meditation every morning and in the afternoon he gave vast and profound teachings to his disciples in order to mature their minds; during the waning moon he concentrated on teaching the three types of vows (vinaya, bodhisattva, and vajrayana) and opened the way to liberation and a higher form of life.

When he knew that he had completed the activities of this life, in order to demonstrate the results of previous karma, he accepted some poison from a man whose mind was ruled by *maras*.[12] His closest attendant then said to him, "This man [who poisoned you] will become fuel for the fires of hell. Who will protect him?" Phagmo Drupa replied, "I will take the responsibility for his deed on myself." Therefore, he assembled the monks and asked them to join him in making offerings and reciting the *khangkani* purification mantras and the rest.[13] Then he meditated on the path of transformation.[14]

In the Iron Tiger Year (1172 C.E.) at the age of 61 he gathered his closest and most faithful attendants and, having completed all the levels of practice, addressed them as follows: "All compounded things are by nature impermanent. Therefore one should make ready the butter and the juniper branch [for the funeral rites]. Do not be attached to wealth; such attachment is the root cause of suffering. Do not follow bad or worldly friends. Practice with bodhicitta, combining loving kindness and compassion. Do not look for faults in others.

"Do not worry about me, I am like a small flying bird. I will be in the eastern buddha-field of Akshobya under the name Bodhisattva Stainless Discrimination. I will be the source of happiness and peace to all beings. Therefore, all of you who have faith in me pray to that place."

On the 25th day of that month, he joined the assembly of monks in the morning and gave his final demonstration. At that time many wondrous signs of his miraculous power appeared, like earthquakes, rainbows, and the aroma of incense. Many relics and seed syllables spontaneously appeared on his body. The minds of those present were strongly affected.

Notes

1. A Tibetan "Hercules" figure.
2. Vinaya: The rules of monastic discipline.
3. Six texts of the Kadampas: six Mahayana texts especially revered by the Kadampas. They are: Buddhajataka; Dharmapada; Bodhicharyavatara; Shiksasamucaya; Bodhisattvabhumi; Shravakabhumi.
4. Galopa: A famous translator who specialized in Chakrasamvara and the four-armed form of Mahakala.
5. Five-deity Chakrasamvara: This version of the *Chakrasamvara Tantra* practice derives from the Indian Mahasiddha Ghantapada and became a speciality of the Drikung Kagyu order.
6. Lam Dre: This practice of the *Hevajra Tantra* derives from the Indian Mahasiddha Virupa andd is a speciality of the Sakyapa order.
7. Shamatha: A practice for one-pointedly calming the mind.
8. Mahamudra: Here, the ultimate reality of the mind; beyond words, it is therefore called merely a great symbol.
9 "Holding the Golden Umbrella": A high monastic rank.
10. Phadampa Sangye: A great Indian mahasiddha who

came to Tibet at the time of Milarepa. They demonstrated miraculous powers to each other. He is the founder of the Zhi Jed system.

11. Zhi Jed: literally means "pacifying" and refers to pacifying mental confusion. It derives from the *Prajnaparamita Sutras*.

12. Mara: A personification of the evil and obscuring forces opposing the bodhisattva's progress.

13. A purification mantra associated with Buddha Akshobya.

14. Path of transformation: transforming negative karmic effects into medicinal ambrosia.

The Life of Jigten Sumgön[1]

Om Svasti.
The victorious Shakya saw the five sights.[2]
He showed the victorious path, and to expand the
teachings took birth again as the victorious Regent,
Ratna Shri.
I prostrate to him.

The glorious Phagmo Drupa[3] had five hundred disciples
who possessed the white umbrella;[4] but, as he said again
and again, his successor would be an *upasaka* who had
attained the tenth level of a bodhisattva. This is the story of
that successor, the peerless Great Lord Drikungpa, Jigten
Sumgön.

Limitless *kalpas* ago, Jigten Sumgön was born as the
Chakravartin Tsibkyi Mukhyu. He was the father of a
thousand princes, but then he renounced the kingdom and
attained enlightenment and was called the Tathagata Lurik
Drönma. Although he had already attained enlightenment,
he appeared later as the Bodhisattva Kunsang Wangkur
Gyalpo. At the time of the Buddha Kashyapa, he appeared
as the potter Gakyong. At the time of the Buddha Shakyamuni, he appeared as the Stainless Licchavi, who was
inseparable from the Buddha himself. Later, he was born as

29

the *Acharya* Nagarjuna.[5] Through these births, he benefited the Buddha's teachings and countless sentient beings.
Then, so that the essence of the Buddha's teachings
might flourish, he was born to a noble family in Tibet. His
father was Naljorpa Dorje, a great practitioner of Yamantaka, and his mother was Rakyisa Tsunma. Many marvelous
signs accompanied the birth. He learned the teachings of
Yamantaka from his father, and became expert in reading
and writing by the age of four. From his uncle, the Abbot
Darma, the great Radreng Gomchen, the Reverend Khorwa Lungkhyer, and others, he learned many sutras and
tantras. At that time, he was called Tsunpa Kyab, and later,
Dorje Pal.

Jigten Sumgön's coming was predicted in many sutras,
tantras, and termas. For example, in the *Yeshe Yongsu
Gyepa Sutra* it is said: "In the northern snow ranges will
appear a being called Ratna Shri. He will benefit my
teachings and be renowned in the three worlds." In the
Gongdü Sutra it is said: "At a place called Dri, the Source of
the Dharma, Ratna Shri will appear in the Year of the Pig.
He will gather a hundred thousand fully ordained monks.
After that, he will go to the Ngönga buddha-field. He will
be called Stainless White Sugata and have a large retinue."
In the *Gyalpo Kaithang* it is said: "From glorious Samye[6] to
the northeast, at a place called Drikung, the source of the
dharma, the Lord-King Trisong Detsen will be born in the
Year of the Pig as the Sugata Ratna Shri. He will gather a
hundred thousand bodhisattvas. He will go to the Ngönga
buddha-field and be called Stainless White Sugata. In that
buddha-field, he will become the fully perfected king."
Thus, he was clearly predicted.

When Jigten Sumgön was still young, his father passed
away. His family's fortunes declined, and he supported his
family by reciting scriptures. Once, he was offered a goat.
As he led it away, it tried to break loose; he pulled back, but
the goat dragged him for a short distance and he left his
footprints in the rock. When he was eight, he had a vision

of Yamantaka. On another occasion, while meditating at Tsib Lungmoche, he saw all the dharmas of samsara and nirvana as insubstantial appearance, like a reflection in a mirror. Even when he was in Kham he was renowned as a yogin. Jigten Sumgön realized the practices of Mahamudra and luminosity, and in his sleep visited the Arakta Padmai buddha-field. As mentioned earlier, from the great Radreng Gomchen he learned all the teachings of the Kadam[8] tradition. From Lama Lhopa Dorje Nyingpo, he received the teachings of Guhyasamaja and others. Once, there was a drought in Kham. He took the food that was offered to him as a fee for his reading and distributed it to those who were starving. Thus, he saved many lives.

Many important people began to approach Jigten Sumgön for teachings. One, Gonda Pandita, who came from Central Tibet, told him about Phagmo Drupa. Just by hearing the name of Phagmo Drupa, Jigten Sumgön's mind was moved like the leaves of a *kengshu* tree are moved by the wind. With great hardship, he traveled from Kham to Central Tibet. A rainbow stretched the length of his journey, and the Protector, Dorje Lekpa, took the forms of a rabbit and a child and attended him, looking after his needs. He came to the dangerous, rocky path of Kyere. There, a natural formation of the six-syllable mantra[9] transformed itself into a vision of the face of Phagmo Drupa.

Jigten Sumgön traveled day and night. On the way, he met a woman and man who said, "We have come from Phagmo Dru." Seeing them as the guru's emanations, he prostrated to them. He arrived at the Phagdru Monastery at midnight, and a Khampa[10] invited him inside. When he met Phagmo Drupa, the guru said, "Now, all of my disciples are present." Jigten Sumgön then offered his teacher a bolt of silk, a bolt of cloth, and his horse — but Phagmo Drupa refused the horse, explaining that he did not accept offerings of animals. Jigten Sumgön also offered a bag of food, and Phagmo Drupa used it to perform a feast-offering to Chakrasamvara. Then, Phagmo Drupa gave Jigten Sumgön the Two-Fold Bodhisattva Vow and the name Bodhisattva Ratna Shri." As one vessel fills another, Phagmo Drupa gave Jigten Sumgön all the teachings of sutra and tantra. At that time, there lived a woman who was an emanation of Vajrayogini. Phagmo Drupa suggested to Taklung Thangpa[12] that he stay with her; but Taklung Thangpa, not wishing to give up his monk's vows, refused, and shortly afterward the emanation passed away. Lingje Repa[13] then fashioned a cup from the woman's skull. This made him late for the assembly, and the food-offerings had already been distributed by the time he got there. Taking the skull-cup, he circulated among the monks, receiving offerings of food from each. The monks gave only small portions, but Phagmo Drupa gave a large amount, filling the skull-cup completely, and Jigten Sumgön gave even more, forming a mound of food which covered the skull-cup like an umbrella. Lingje Repa then walked again through the assembly, and as he walked he spontaneously composed and sang a song of praise in twenty verses. Finally, he stopped in front of Jigten Sumgön, offering the food — and the song — to him.

One day, Phagmo Drupa wanted to see if any special signs would arise concerning his three closest disciples, and he gave each of them a foot of red cloth with which to make a meditation hat. Taklung Thangpa used only what he had. Lingje Repa added a piece of cotton cloth to the front of his hat, and Jigten Sumgön added a second foot of cloth to his, making it much larger. This was considered very auspicious. On another occasion, Phagmo Drupa called Jigten Sumgön and Taklung Thangpa and said, "I think that the Tsangpo River is overflowing today. Please go and see." Both disciples saw the river following its normal course, and returned; but Jigten Sumgön, thinking there was some purpose in the guru's question, told him, "The river has overflowed, and Central Tibet and Kham are now both underwater." This foretold the flourishing of Jigten Sumgön's activities, and he became known as a master of interdependent origination.[14]

At this time, in accordance with the prediction made by Phagmo Drupa, Jigten Sumgön still held only the vows of an upasaka. One day, Phagmo Drupa asked him to remain behind after the assembly and instructed him to sit in the seven-point posture of Vairochana.[15] Touching him on his head, throat, and heart-centers, he said, "Om, Ah, Hum" three times and told him, "You will be a great meditator, and I rejoice."

Jigten Sumgön attended Phagmo Drupa for two years and six months. During that time, he received all of his guru's teachings and was told that he would be his successor. At the time of Phagmo Drupa's *parinirvana*, a radiant five-pronged golden *vajra* emanated from his heart-center and dissolved into the heart-center of Jigten Sumgön, this being seen by the other disciples. Jigten Sumgön then gave all his belongings to benefit the monastery and to help build the memorial stupa for his guru.

After this, he met many other teachers. From Dakpo Gomtsul[16] he received the Four Yogas of Mahamudra. A patroness then promised him provisions for three years and Jigten Sumgön, earnestly wishing to practice the teachings he had received, retired to the Echung Cave to meditate. In those three years, he gained a rough understanding of the outer, inner, and secret aspects of interdependent origination. He then realized that the cause of wandering in samsara is the difficulty *prana* has in entering the *avadhuti*, and so he practiced on prana, saw many buddhas and bodhisattvas face-to-face, and had visions of his mind purifying the six realms.[17] Then he went on a pilgrimage to Phagmo Dru and other holy places.

On his return to the Echung Cave, he practiced with one-pointed mind. In the same way that maras arose as obstacles to Lord Buddha at the time of his enlightenment, and Tsering Chenga and others tried to hinder Milarepa, the final fruition of his karma then arose, and he contracted leprosy. Becoming intensely depressed, he thought, "Now, I should die in this solitary place and transfer my consciousness." He prostrated to an image of Avalokiteshvara that had been blessed many times by Phagmo Drupa. At the first prostration, he thought, "Among sentient beings, I am the worst." At the second, he thought, "I have all the teachings of my guru, including the instructions of *bardo* and the transference of consciousness, and need have no fear of death." Then, remembering that other beings didn't have these teachings, strong compassion arose in him. In that state of mind, he sat down and generated compassionate thoughts toward others. His sickness left him, like clouds blown away from the sun, and at that moment he attained Buddhahood. He had practiced at the Echung Cave for seven years.

Shortly after this, he had a vision of the Seven Taras. Because he had a full understanding of interdependent origination, and had realized the unity of discipline (*shila*) and Mahamudra, he took the vows of a fully-ordained monk. From this time, Jigten Sumgön did not eat meat. As he had already been named Phagmo Drupa's successor, the chief monks of his guru's monastery invited him to return.

After taking the abbot's seat at the monastery, Jigten Sumgön insisted on a strict observance of monastic discipline. One day, some monks said, "We are the 'nephews' of Milarepa and should be allowed to drink *chang*." Saying this, they drank. When Jigten Sumgön counseled them, they replied, "You yourself should keep the discipline of not harming others." Phagmo Drupa then appeared in a vision to Jigten Sumgön and said to him, "Leave this old, silken seat and go to the north. There you will benefit many sentient beings."

Jigten Sumgön went north, and on the way, at Nyenchen Thanglha, he was greeted by the protector of that place. At Namra, a spirit-king and his retinue took the upasaka vow from him, and Jigten Sumgön left one of his foot-prints behind for them as an object of devotion. He gave meditation instruction to vultures flying overhead, and they practiced according to those teachings. Once, at a word from Jigten Sumgön, a horse that was running away returned to him. He also sent an emanation of himself to pacify a war in Bodhgaya[18] begun by Duruka tribesmen.

On another occasion, at Dam, he gave teachings and received many offerings. At the end of a day which had seemed very long, he told the crowd, "Now, go immediately to your homes," and suddenly it was just before dawn of the next day. To finish his talk. Jigten Sumgön had stopped the sun. When he was at Namra Mountain, Brahma, the king of the gods, requested the vast and profound teachings. On the way to Drikung, the great god Barlha received him. The children of Jenthang built a throne for him, and he sat there and instructed the people of that town. Even the water, which has no mind, listened to his teachings and made the sound, *Nagarjuna.*

Then he came to Drikung Thel. In his thirty-seventh year, he established Drikung Jangchub Ling, and appointed Pön Gompa Dorje Senge as supervisor for the construction of the monastery. Many monks gathered there and enjoyed the rainfall of the profound dharma.

In Tibet, there are nine great protectors of the dharma. Among them, Barlha, Sogra, Chuphen Luwang, Terdrom Menmo, and Namgyal Karpo bowed down at Jigten Sumgön's feet, took the upasaka vow, and promised to protect the teachings and practitioners of the Drikung lineage.

At one time, water was very scarce in Drikung. Jigten Sumgön gave 108 turquoise to his attendant, Rinchen Drak, with instructions to hide them in various places. Rinchen Drak hid all but one, which he kept for himself and put in his robe. The turquoise he hid became sources of water, and the one he kept turned into a frog. Startled, he threw it away, and in falling it became blind in one eye. Where the frog landed, a stream arose which was called Chumik Shara. Most of these streams were dried up by fire when Drikung Thel was destroyed during the middle of the fourteenth century, but some still remain.

Twice a month, on the new and full moon, Jigten Sumgön and his monks observed a purification ceremony called Sojong. Once, some monks arrived late and Jigten Sumgön decided to discontinue the practice, but Brahma requested him to maintain that tradition, and he agreed.

Jigten Sumgön continued to look after Densa Thel, his old monastery. Once, the *dakinis* brought an assembly of 2,800 yidams on a net of horse-hair and presented them to him. To the memory of Phagmo Drupa, he built an auspicious stupa of many doors and placed those yidams inside, with a door for each of them; and from this there came down the tradition of building stupas of this type. He also visited Daklha Gampo, the monastery of Gampopa. From Gampopa's image, light-rays streamed forth, merging inseparably with Jigten Sumgön, and he attained both the ordinary and extraordinary *siddhis* of the treasure of space. In a vision, he met with Ananda[19] and discussed the teachings.

Once, Lama Shang[20] said, "This year, the dakinis of Oddiyana will come to invite me and the Great Drikungpa to join them. He is a master of interdependent origination and won't have to go there, but I should go." Soon after this, the dakinis came for him and he passed away; but when they came to invite Jigten Sumgön, he refused to go, and the dakinis changed their prayer of invitation into a supplication for the guru's longevity. Then all the *dakas* and dakinis made offerings to him and promised to guide his disciples.

Jigten Sumgön had many important students, among them the two Chengas, the Great Abbot Gurawa, Nyö Gyalwa Lhanangpa,[21] Gar Chöding, Palchen Chöye, Drubtob Nyakse, the two Tsang-tsangs, and others. These were the leaders of the philosophers. The vinaya-holders were Thakma Düldzin, Dakpo Düldzin, and others. The Kadampa *geshes* were Kyo Dorje Nyingpo and others. The

translators were Nup, Phakpa, and others. The leaders of
the *tantrikas* were Tre, Ngok, and others. The leaders of the
yogins were Düdsi, Belpo, and others. When Jigten Sumgön taught, rainbows appeared and gods rained flowers
from the sky. Machen Pomra and other protectors listened
to his teachings, and the kings of Tibet, India, and China
were greatly devoted to him. At this time, Jigten Sumgön
had 55,525 followers. To feed this ocean of disciples, Mat-
rö, the King of the Nagas and the source of all the wealth of
Jambudvipa, acted as patron for the monastery.

Near Drikung Thel there was a rock called Lion-
Shoulder, which Jigten Sumgön saw as the mandala of
Chakrasamvara. He established a monastery there and, to
spread the teachings and benefit sentient beings, built
another auspicious stupa of many doors, using a special
method. He also repaired Samye Monastery.

Jigten Sumgön's main yidam practice was the Chakrasamvara of Five Deities, and he sometimes manifested in
that form in order to work with those who were difficult to
train. When a war began in Minyak, in Eastern Tibet, he
protected the people there through his miracle-power. The
number of his disciples increased to 70,000. Many of the
brightest of these attained enlightenment in one lifetime,
while those of lesser intelligence attained various *bhumis*,
and everyone else realized at least the nature of his or her
own mind.

In one of the predictions about Jigten Sumgön, it was
said, "A hundred thousand incarnate *(tulku)* great beings
will gather." Here, "tulku" meant that they would be
monks and have perfect discipline, and "great beings"
meant that they would all be bodhisattvas. In other life-
stories, it is said that in an instant Jigten Sumgön visited all
the buddha-fields, saw buddhas like Amitabha and
Akshobya, and listened to their teachings. Jigten Sumgön
himself said that whoever so much as heard his name and
had the chance to go to Layel, in Drikung, would be freed
from birth in the lower realms, and that whoever suppli-

cated him — whether from near or far away — would be blessed, and his or her meditation would grow more firm. He also said that all sentient beings living in the mountains of Drikung, even the ants, would not be born again in lower realms.

From the essence of the instructions of sutra and tantra, Jigten Sumgön gave teachings which were compiled by his disciple Chenga Sherab Jungne into a text called *Gong Chik*, which has 150 topics and 40 appendices.

A naga-king named Meltro Zichen once went to Drikung for teachings. Jigten Sumgön sent a message to his disciples to remain in seclusion so that those with miracle-power would not harm the naga and those without such power would not be harmed themselves. The message was given to everyone but the *Mahasiddha* Gar Dampa, who was meditating in the depths of a long cave. When the naga arrived, he made a loud noise which was heard even by Gar Dampa. He came out to see what was happening, and saw a frightening, dark-blue snake whose length circled the monastery three times and whose head looked in at the window of Jigten Sumgön's palace. Without examining the situation, he thought that the naga was there to harm his guru, and he manifested as a giant *garuda* which chased the naga away. At Rölpa Trang, there is a smooth and clear print left by the naga, and at Dermo Mik there is a very clear mark left by the garuda when it landed on a rock. Near the river of Khyung-Ngar Gel, there are marks left by both the garuda and the naga.

A Ceylonese arhat, a follower of the Buddha, once heard that *Mahapandita* Shakya Shri Bhadra was going to Tibet, and he gave that teacher's brother a white lotus, asking that he give it to the Mahapandita to give to Nagarjuna in Tibet. When Shakya Shri Bhadra arrived in Tibet, he ordained many monks but didn't know where to find Nagarjuna. When giving ordination, he would distribute robes, and once an ordinary disciple of Jigten Sumgön approached him for ordination and then asked for a robe, but none were left. He insisted strongly. One of Shakya Shri Bhadra's attendants pushed him away and he fell, causing blood to come from his nose. Before this, Shakya Shri Bhadra had been accustomed to seeing Tara in the morning when he recited the seven-branch prayer,[22] but for six days after this incident she didn't show herself. Then, on the seventh day, she appeared with her back turned to him. "What have I done wrong?" he asked her. "Your attendant beat a disciple of Nagarjuna," she replied, "and brought blood from his nose." When he asked how he could purify this misdeed, Tara told him, "Make as many dharma-robes as you have years, and offer them to fully-ordained monks who have no robes." Shakya Shri Bhadra then searched for the monk who had been turned away. When he found him, and learned the name of his teacher, he realized that Jigten Sumgön was Nagarjuna's incarnation. He sent one of his attendants to offer the white lotus to Jigten Sumgön. In return, Jigten Sumgön sent many offerings of his own and asked that Shakya Shri Bhadra visit Drikung, but the Mahapandita could not go there, though he sent many verses of praise. Because Nagarjuna had knowingly taken birth as Jigten Sumgön in order to dispel wrong views, and was teaching at Drikung, Shakya Shri Bhadra saw that there was no need to go there.

At this time, many lesser *panditas* were visiting Tibet. One of them, named Bi Bhuti Chandra, said, "Let us talk with the Kadampas; the followers of Mahamudra[23] tell lies." Shakya Shri Bhadra said to him, "Don't say that," and recounted the above story. "Because Jigten Sumgön is a great teacher," he continued, "you should now apologize for having said these things." Bi Bhuti Chandra then went to Drikung, made full apology, and constructed an image of Chakrasamvara at Sinpori Mountain.

One day, a great scholar named Dru Kyamo came to Drikung from Sakya to debate with Jigten Sumgön. When he saw the guru's face he saw him as the Buddha himself, and his two chief disciples — Chenga Sherab Jungne and Chenga Drakpa Jungne — as Shariputra and Maudgalyayana. There was no way he could debate with Jigten Sumgön after this. His devotion blossomed fully, and he became one of Jigten Sumgön's principal disciples. Later he was called Ngorje Repa and wrote a text called *Thegchen Tenpai Nyingpo* as a commentary on Jigten Sumgön's teachings. The number of Jigten Sumgön's disciples continued to increase. At one rainy-season retreat, 100,000 "morality-sticks" were distributed to count the monks attending. Not long after that, 2,700 monks were sent to Lachi and equal numbers were sent to Tsari and Mount Kailash, but by the next year 130,000 monks had again gathered at Drikung. Karmapa Düsum Khyenpa[24] once came to Drikung after visiting Daklha Gampo. At Bam Thang, Jigten Sumgön and his disciples received him warmly. At that time, Karmapa saw Jigten Sumgön as the Buddha, and his two chief disciples as Shariputra and Maudgalyayana surrounded by *arhats*. When they returned to the main assembly hall, the Serkhang, Karmapa again saw Jigten Sumgön as the Buddha, with his two disciples appearing as Maitreya and Manjushri surrounded by bodhisattvas. Thus, Düsum Khyenpa showed great devotion and received many teachings. He also saw the entire area of Drikung as the mandala of Chakrasamvara.

The question arose of who would hold the lineage after Jigten Sumgön's passing. Jigten Sumgön had confidence in many of his disciples, but had thought for a long time that the succession should pass to one of his family clan, the Drugyal Kyura. Since he had been born in Kham, he sent one of his disciples, Palchen Shri Phukpa, there to teach his family members. Displaying miracle-power and proclaiming his guru's reputation, Palchen Shri Phukpa taught Jigten Sumgön's uncle Könchog Rinchen and his uncle's son, Anye Atrak, and grandsons. Their minds became attracted, and they moved to Central Tibet. Their stories are told in the *Golden Rosary of the Drikung Kagyu*.

One day, Jigten Sumgön told his disciple Gar Chöding to go to the Soksam Bridge and offer *torma* to the nagas living in the water. "You will receive special wealth," he told him. A naga-king named Sokma Me offered Gar Chöding a tooth of the Buddha and three special gems. Generally, it is said that this tooth had been taken by the naga-king Dradrok as an object of devotion. This was the same naga who usually lived in the area of Magadha, but had access to Soksam by way of an underwater gate. Gar Chöding offered the tooth and gems to Jigten Sumgön, who said, "It is good to return wealth to its owner," indicating that the tooth had once been his own. "As you are wealthy," he continued, "you should make an image of me and put the tooth in its heart." A skilled Chinese artisan was then invited to build the statue, and the tooth was enshrined there as a relic. Jigten Sumgön consecrated this statue hundreds of times. It was kept in the Serkhang and called Serkhang Chöje (Dharma Lord of Serkhang). Its power of blessings was regarded as being equal to that of Jigten Sumgön himself. It spoke to many shrine-keepers, and to a lama named Dawa it taught the Six Yogas of Naropa. Later, when Drikung was destroyed by fire, it was buried in the sand for protection. When the Drikung Kyabgön returned to rebuild the monastery, a search was made for the statue, which came out of the sand by itself, saying, "Here I am." Thus, this image possessed great power. Gar Chöding made many other images of Jigten Sumgön at this time.

Jigten Sumgön had by now grown old, and could not travel often to Densa Thel. He sent Chenga Drakpa Jungne there as his Vajra Regent, and that disciple's activities were very successful. Under the leadership of Panchen Guya Khangpa, Jigten Sumgön sent 55,525 disciples to stay at Mount Kailash. Under Geshe Yakru Paldrak, 55,525 were sent to Lachi. Under Dordzin Gowoche, 55,525 were sent to Tsari. Even at the time of Chungpo Dorje Drakpa, the fourth successor to Jigten Sumgön, there were 180,000 disciples at Drikung.

Once, Jigten Sumgön went to the Dorje Lhokar Cave. "This cave is too small," he said, and stretched, causing the inside of the cave to expand, and leaving the imprint of his clothes on the rock. Because the cave was dark, he pushed a stick through the rock, making a window. He then made shelves in the rock to hold his belongings. All of these can be seen very clearly. Jigten Sumgön also left many footprints in the four directions of the area of Drikung.

One day, Jigten Sumgön fell ill. Phagmo Drupa appeared to him in a vision and explained a yogic technique by means of which he became well again. Jigten Sumgön taught according to the needs of his disciples. To some, according to their disposition, he gave instructions in the practice of the Eight Herukas of the Nyingma[25] tradition.

Toward the end of his life, he predicted a period of decline for the Drikung lineage. Taking a small stick that he used to clean his teeth, he planted it in the ground and said, "When this stick has reached a certain height, I will return." This foretold the coming of Gyalwa Kunga Rinchen. Jigten Sumgön then asked Chenga Sherab Jungne to be his successor, but the latter declined out of modesty. Then he asked the great abbot Gurawa Tsültrim Dorje, and he agreed.

In order to encourage lazy ones to the dharma, at the age of seventy-five, in the Year of the Fire-Ox, Jigten Sumgön entered parinirvana. His body was cremated on the thirteenth day of the month of Vaishaka. Gods created clouds of offerings. Flowers rained from the sky to the level of one's knees. His skull was untouched by the fire, and his brain appeared as the mandala of the Sixty-Two Deities of Chakrasamvara, which was more clear than if a skilled artist had made it. His heart was also not touched by the fire, and was found to have turned a golden color. This showed that he was an incarnation of the Buddha. Likewise, countless relics appeared.

After Jigten Sumgön's passing, most of the funerary responsibilities were taken on by Chenga Sherab Jungne, even though he had earlier declined the succession. He went to Senge Phungpa Mountain to view the mandala of

Chakrasamvara, saw Jigten Sumgön there, and thus thought that he should build a memorial in that place. Jigten Sumgön then again appeared in a vision on the mountain of the Samadhi Cave and said to him, "Son, do as you wish, but also follow my intention." Then he disappeared. Doing as he wished, Chenga Sherab Jungne built an auspicious stupa of many doors called "Sage, Overpowerer of the Three Worlds." In that stupa, he put Jigten Sumgön's heart and many other relics. Following his guru's intention, he built the stupa "Body-Essence, Ornament of the World," which was made of clay mixed with jewel-dust, saffron, and various kinds of incense. In that stupa, he put Jigten Sumgön's skull and brain, along with many other relics including Vinaya texts brought from India by Atisha, and the *100,000-Verse Prajnaparamita*.

Jigten Sumgön now abides in the Eastern Great All-Pervading Buddha-Field, surrounded by limitless numbers of disciples from this earth who died with strong devotion to him. When such people die, they will be born there immediately. Jigten Sumgön will place his hand on their heads, blessing them and welcoming them there.

Notes

1. Jigten Sumgön (1143-1217) was the founder of the Drikung Kagyü lineage. This abridged account of this life is taken from the *Golden Rosary of the Drikung Kagyu*, by the Fourth Drikung Kyabgön, Chetsang Rinpoche, Tendzin Pemai Gyaltsen. The Drikung Kyabgön is the official head of the Drikung Kagyu lineage.

2. The five sights seen by Buddha Shakyamuni before his descent from the Tushita Heaven: his clan, his country, the time, his family line, and the woman who would be his mother.

3. Phagmo Drupa was the teacher of Jigten Sumgön and a principal disciple of Gampopa, the lineage-succesor of Milarepa and founder of the monastic tradition of the Kagyu lineage.

4. A symbol of great accomplishment.

5. The great Indian Mahayana teacher who lived approximately a thousand years before the time of Jigten Sumgön.

6. The first Buddhist monastery in Tibet.

7. The easternmost province of Tibet.

8. The school following the teachings of the great Indian teacher Atisha and his Tibetan disciple Dromtönpa.

9. The mantra of Avalokiteshvara: OM MANI PADME HUM.

44

10. A person from Kham.

11. Later, Phagmo Drupa also called him Je Jigten Sumgön, meaning "Protector of the Three Worlds," and Kyobpa Rinpoche, "Precious Protector."

12. Taklung Thangpa (1142-1209) was a principal disciple of Phagmo Drupa and founder of the Taklung Kagyu lineage, one of the "eight lesser" schools of the Kagyu tradition.

13. Lingje Repa (1128-1188) was a principal disciple of Phagmo Drupa. His student, Tsangpa Gyare, founded the Drukpa Kagyu lineage, another of the "eight lesser" schools.

14. Because Jigten Sumgön was familiar with the workings of interdependent origination, he knew how to create auspicious situations by an appropriate statement or action.

15. A meditation posture in which one sits with one's legs crossed with the feet resting on opposite thighs, back straight, eyes gazing downward at a slant, chin drawn in, shoulders raised, tongue raised to palate, and hands resting in the samadhi-gesture in the lap.

16. Dakpo Gomtsul was the nephew of Gampopa and his successor as Abbot of Daklha Gampo Monastery.

17. The six realms of samsara; those of gods, jealous gods, human beings, animals, hungry ghosts, and hell-beings.

18. The site of the Buddha's enlightenment in India.

19. Buddha Shakyamuni's cousin, disciple, and personal attendant.

20. Lama Shang (1123-1193) was a disciple of Dakpo Gomtsul and founder of the Tsalpa Kagyu lineage, one of the "four greater" schools.

21. A previous incarnation of Jamgön Kongtrul the Great.

22. A standard Mahayana liturgy, consisting of verses of praise, offering, confession, rejoicing, requesting teaching, requesting teachers to remain, and dedication of merit.

23. In other words, the Kagyudpas.

24. Karmapa Düsum Khyenpa (1110-1193) was a principal disciple of Gampopa and founder of the Karma Kagyu lineage, one of the "four greater" schools.

25. The school following the teachings of Padmasambhava, Shantirakshita, and Vimalamitra. The oldest lineage of Buddhism in Tibet.

Supplication to the Lineage Gurus

Könchog Trinlay Sangpo (the 25th successor of Jigten Sumgön and the second incarnation of the Drikung Kyabgön, Chetsang Rinpoche) composed this dedication prayer to the Drikung lineage gurus.

Precious guru who possesses the three kindnesses,[1]
your name is renowned as the Drikungpa.
Generally, whatever peace and happiness there are
    in samsara and nirvana
come from supplicating you, Lord.

On the crown of my head, on a sun and moon seat,
kind root guru,
I supplicate you.

In the Dharma Palace of Ogmin,
great Vajradhara the Dharmakaya,
I supplicate you.

In the east, in Sahor, in the Palace of the King,
Tilli Prajnabhadra,
I supplicate you.

In the north, in the monastery of Phullahari,
learned Mahapandita Naropa,

I supplicate you.

In the south, in the monastery of Drowo Lung,
translator Marpa Lotsawa,
I supplicate you.

In the hermitage of the Lachi snow range,
Mila Shepa Dorje,
I supplicate you.

In the east, at the mountain of jewels, Gampo,
Lord King of Physicians,
I supplicate you.

In glorious Thatsa,[2] the source of the dharma,
Lord Self-Born Buddha,
I supplicate you.

In Drisewa, at Jangchub Ling,
kind Lords of Dharma,
I supplicate you.

In Gura, the Monastery of the Dharma,
Great Abbot Tsültrim Dorje,
I supplicate you.

In the northern Vajrasana,[3]
great nephew Sönam Drakpa,
I supplicate you.

At the two Dharma Thrones, Dri and Den,[4]
Chenga Dorje Drakpa,
I supplicate you.

In the unchanging Vajra Palace,
Chungpo Dorje Drakpa —
I supplicate you.

In the Glorious Palace of Great Bliss,
Thokha Rinchen Senge,
I supplicate you.

In the Pure Monastery, free from elaboration,

Tsamche Drakpa Sönam,
I supplicate you.

In Ogmin, in the Lhündrub Monastery,
Chunyi Dorje Rinchen,
I supplicate you.

In the Palace of Tashi Phüntsok,
Tulku Dorje Gyalpo,
I supplicate you.

In the Dakpa Rabjam Monastery,
Omniscient Chökyi Gyalpo,[5]
I supplicate you.

In the Palace of Tsekha Deden,
Spiritual Friend Döndrub Gyalpo,
I supplicate you.

In China, at the Five-Peaked Mountain,
Lord Dakpo Wang,
I supplicate you.

In the Palace of Unification and Equanimity,
Dharma King Rinchen Palsang,
I supplicate you.

In the Dharmakaya Palace of the Innate,
Rinchen Chökyi Gyaltsen,
I supplicate you.

In the Palace of the Self-Born Emanation,
Rinchen Chökyi Gyalpo,
I supplicate you.

In the Palace of Unchanging Bodhi,
Gyalwang Kunga Rinchen,
I supplicate you.

In the secret place, Ter Tro, in the upper [country
    of] Sho,
the one called Gyalwang Ratna,
I supplicate you.

In the Palace of Phagmo Tse,
Mahapandita Palgyi Gyatso,
I supplicate you.

In the Firm Vajra Palace,
peerless Chögyal Phüntsok,
I supplicate you.

In the Vajra Palace of Great Bliss,
Great Abbot Namjom Phüntsok,
I supplicate you.

In the second Phullahari,
Mahasiddha Tashi Phüntsok,
I supplicate you.

In Kunga Rawa, in Sho,
Jetsün Könchok Ratna,[6]
I supplicate you.

At the peak of the Supreme Vajra of the Secret
    Mantra,
Vidyadhara Chökyi Drakpa,[7]
I supplicate you.

At the glorious cave of Miyel,
Könchok Trinlay Namgyal,
I supplicate you.

In the Dharma Palace of the Supreme Yana,
Protector Trinlay Sangpo,[8]
I supplicate you.

In the Palace of Dershi Rabgye,
Trinlay Döndrub Chögyal,
I supplicate you.

At the top of Tashi Tsuk,
Lord Könchok Tendzin Drodül,
I supplicate you.

At the Hermitage of Unchanging Bodhi,
Protector Chökyi Gyaltsen,

I supplicate you.

At the hermitage, the Place of Unchanging
    Happiness,
peerless Chökyi Nyima,
I supplicate you.

In the Monastery of Dharmata, which is wherever
    you stay,
kind Pemai Gyaltsen,
I supplicate you.

In the state of self-awareness, which is great bliss,
Tendzin Chökyi Gyaltsen,
I supplicate you.

At Nyin Dzong, the supreme place of Mahayana,
Great Regent Maha Mandzi,
I supplicate you.

In the Palace of Happy Sunlight,
Rinchen Tenpai Dzegyen,
I supplicate you.

In the Dharma Palace of Omniscience,
supremely victorious Tukje Nyima,
I supplicate you.

In the ancient Dharma Fortress of Shedrub,
Vidyadhara Nuden Dorje,
I supplicate you.

In the glorious monastery of Jangchub Ling,
Jetsün Könchok Chökyab,
I supplicate you.

At the peak of the Dharmachakra of the Supreme
    Yana,
peerless Chökyi Lodrö,
I supplicate you.

In the supreme state of great bliss and luminosity,

Supreme Guide Shiwai Lodrö,
I supplicate you.

On the crown of my head, on a sun and moon seat,
kind root guru,
I supplicate you.

Please bless the beings of the six realms.[9]
Please bless them so they may be ripened and freed.
May they reverse attachment to objects of desire.
May their kleshas be self-liberated.
May their bodies be transformed into deities.
May they realize their voice as inseparable from
    mantra.
May they realize their mind as Dharmakaya.
As in the life-stories of the former Lord Gurus,
please bless me so my life-span and realization may
    come together.
Please bless me so I may practice loving-kindness
    and compassion
toward all mother beings, filling space.
May all appearances of samsara and nirvana
be realized as the equal taste of Mahamudra.

(This was written by the Drikung Vande, Trinlay Sangpo,
at the request of the glorious Trinlay Gyurme at Thagön.)

Notes

1. The granting of empowerment, transmission, and oral instructions.
2. Phagdru, the country where Phagmo Drupa lived and taught.
3. Drikung.
4. Drikung and Densa Thel (the monastery of Phagmo Drupa).
5. One of the principal teachers of Tsongkhapa, and the guru from whom many practices of the Kagyü lineage passed into the Gelugpa tradition.
6. The first Chetsang Drikung Kyabgön.
7. The first Chungtsang Drikung Kyabgön. (The Chetsang and Chungtsang incarnations have served alternately as Drikung Kyabgön.)
8. This is the guru who is named as the author of this prayer. The remaining supplications were written by later teachers.
9. Gods, jealous gods, humans, animals, hungry ghosts, and hell beings.

The Song on Attaining Enlightenment

At the age of thirty-five, Jigten Sumgön attained enlightenment at the Echung Cave and sang this song:

In three nights and four days,
my karma and obscurations were purified.
I realized the cause and effect of interdependent
    origination.
The treasure of the profound tantra revealed itself.
In the oneness of the great luminosity,
the two fixations of meditation and activity were
    purified!
I recognize that I am [now] a lord of yogins.

Notes

1. Because of the indestructible nature of awakened mind, the boundaries between meditation and the post-meditation experience have completely disappeared.

The Song of the Five Profound Paths of Mahamudra

These teachings were given to Jigten Sumgön by Phagmo Drupa. On obtaining certainty in them, Jigten Sumgön sang this song:

> I bow at the feet of glorious Phagmo Drupa.
>
> If the steed of love and compassion
> does not run for the benefit of others,
> it will not be rewarded in the assembly of gods and
> men.
> Attend, therefore, to the preliminaries.
>
> If one's body, the King of Deities,
> is not stabilized on this unchanging ground,
> the retinue of dakinis will not assemble.
> Be sure, therefore, of your body as the yidam.
>
> If on the guru, snow mountain of the four kayas,
> the sun of devotion fails to shine,
> the stream of blessings will not arise.
> Attend, therefore, to this mind of devotion.
>
> If from the sky-like expanse of Mind-as-such[1]

the clouds of preconception are not blown away,
the planets and stars of the two wisdoms[2] will not
  shine.
Attend, therefore, to this mind without
  preconception.

If the wish-fulfilling gem of the two accumulations[3]
is not polished by aspiration,
the results we have hoped for will not arise.
Attend, therefore, to this final dedication.[4]

Notes

1. Naked mind, free from grasping and fixation.

2. The wisdoms which perceive the full range of things to be known and the particular qualities of each.

3. The accumulations of merit and wisdom, which lead to Buddhahood.

4. The Mahayana practice of dedicating, at the end of any practice session, one's merit for the benefit of others.

The Song at Tsa-Uk Dzong-Drom

In order to open this secret place, and to inspire the exertion of his disciples, Jigten Sumgön went to Tsa-Uk Dzong-Drom and sang this song:

I bow at the feet of glorious Phagmo Drupa.

By the great kindness of glorious Phagmo Drupa,
certainty was born in my mind.
I obtained the confidence of bodhicitta.
I, a yogin, remain in solitude.

My experience and realization come out in words.[1]
[Even] for you disciples who are proper vessels,
experience and realization are difficult.
I, a yogin, remain in solitude.

My qualities have become a source of wealth
that provokes attachment and aggression [in
others].
Consuming the food of Mara is a cause of many
faults.[2]
I, a yogin, remain in solitude.

My attendants are distracted.
It is not helpful to keep bad company.

There is no end to the actions of attachment and
  aggression.
I, a yogin, remain in solitude.

My monks are insincere.
Many think about the needs of this life and the
  next.
Feeding a retinue of cattle is a cause of many faults.
I, a yogin, remain in solitude.

My actions have been [only] for this life.
I [only] aspire to worldly dharmas.
This deceives faithful disciples.
I, a yogin, remain in solitude.

A phantom crosses a mirage-river.
Dream-bees sip a sky-lotus.
The son of a barren woman plays music and sings.
Those who are childish, and have no experience or
  realization,
say that through worldly activities one can realize
  the absolute truth.

[But] one's pure and stainless mind
abides with the precious teachings
on the mountain of non-duality.
The forest of great bliss grows dense.
The wild animals of recollection and mindfulness
  roam about.
They consume the grass and water
of bliss, clarity, and non-thought.

If you desire solitude, practice in this way.
I, a yogin, remain in solitude.

Notes

1. Here, Jigten Sumgön is expressing his concern that he has become a mere lecturer, and that no one is taking his teachings to heart.

2. Mara is the personification of obstacles to one's practice. Thus, this line refers to behavior that "feeds" grasping and neurosis.

Supplication to the Kagyu Gurus for the Mist of Great Blessings[1]

The great Nagarjuna was one who realized the profound Emptiness free from extremes. His coming was foretold in many sutras by the Tathagata, and he was reborn as the meditating bhikshu Rinchen Pal, the Protector of the Three Worlds, the Great Drikungpa. Once, he was staying at Jangchub Ling in Drisewa when there was a great drought in that region. All the patrons and monks supplicated and requested him [to end the drought]. In response, he said to Düdsi Shikpo, "Come here. Chant this song of mine near the spring behind our monastery and rain will fall." Thus he composed this song:

Namo Guru!

In the vast sky of the glorious Dharmadhatu,
you pervade all dharmas without limitation of
    boundary or center.
Remembering again and again great Vajradhara the
    Dharmakaya,
I supplicate you with one-pointed mind full of
    yearning.

Guru! Grant your blessings so that I may be realized like you.

Clouds gather in the east over the land of Sahor.
Billowing mists of blessings arise.
Remembering again and again Tilo Prajnabhadra,
I supplicate you with one-pointed mind full of yearning.
Guru! Grant your blessings so that I may be realized like you.

Red lightning flashes over Pushpahari in the north.
You underwent twelve trials for the sake of the dharma.
Remembering again and again learned Mahapandita Naropa,
I supplicate you with one-pointed mind full of yearning.
Guru! Grant your blessings so that I may be realized like you.

The turquoise dragon thunders over the valley of Drowo Lung in the south.
You translated the teachings of the Hearing Lineage into Tibetan.
Remembering again and again the great translator Marpa Lotsawa,
I supplicate you with one-pointed mind full of yearning.
Guru! Grant your blessings so that I may be realized like you.

A gentle rain is falling in the highlands of the Lachi snow range.
The instructions of the Hearing Lineage flow together into a lake.
Remembering again and again glorious Shepa Dorje,
I supplicate you with one-pointed mind full of yearning.

Guru! Grant your blessings so that I may be realized
like you.

The earth is soaked in the Daklha Gampo hills in
the east by the continuous stream of the waters of
Clear Light.
Remembering again and again the Lord, the King
of Physicians,
I supplicate you with one-pointed mind full of
yearning.
Guru! Grant your blessings so that I may be realized
like you.

Shoots sprout in the land of Phagmo Dru.
You opened the treasure of the profound secret
tantra.
Remembering again and again the Lord, the
Self-Born Buddha,
I supplicate you with one-pointed mind full of
yearning.
Guru! Grant your blessings so that I may be realized
like you.

The six grains ripen in the region of Drikung in the
north.
These six grains pervade all six realms.
Remembering again and again the kind Lords of
Dharma,
I supplicate you with one-pointed mind full of
yearning.
Guru! Grant your blessings so that I may be realized
like you.

On the crown of my head, on a sun and moon seat,
sits my kind root guru, inseparable from glorious
Vajradhara.
Remembering you again and again,
I supplicate with one-pointed mind full of yearning.
Guru! Grant your blessings so that I may be realized
like you.

Notes

This translation was prepared by the Venerable Lama Sönam Jorphel and the translator Ngawang Tsering at Drikung Ngaden Chöling in Medabach, West Germany. The prose introduction was written by Karmapa Mikyö Dorje.

The Song of the Six Confidences

Taklung Thangpa, seeing the inconceivable increase of Jigten Sumgön's activities, sent offerings to him and said, "I
have further teachings given by our guru, Phagmo Drupa;
it would be of great benefit if you were to receive these." In
reply, Jigten Sumgön sent offerings of his own, including
this song:

> I bow at the feet of glorious Phagmo Drupa.
>
> By the great kindness of glorious Phagmo Drupa,
> I experienced bliss.
> I obtained the confidence of bodhicitta.
>
> I, a yogin, realized the unity
> of view, meditation, and action.
> There are no sessions to practice.
> In non-effort, I, the yogin, am happy.
> This happy yogin experiences joy.
> This experience of joy is the guru's kindness.
>
> I, a yogin, realized the unity
> of the guru, my own mind, and the Buddha.
> I have no need of superficial devotion.
> In non-effort, I, the yogin, am happy.

This happy yogin experiences joy.
This experience of joy is the guru's kindness.

I, a yogin, realized the unity
of parents, yidams, and the six types of beings.
There is no need for the [superficial] benefit of
    others.
In non-effort, I, the yogin, am happy.
This happy yogin experiences joy.
This experience of joy is the guru's kindness.

I, a yogin, realized the unity
of the sutras, the tantras, and their commentaries.
I have no need of written texts.
In non-effort, I, the yogin, am happy.
This happy yogin experiences joy.
This experience of joy is the guru's kindness.

I, a yogin, realized the unity
of this life, the next, and the bardo.
There is no boundary of death.
In non-effort, I, the yogin, am happy.
This happy yogin experiences joy.
This experience of joy is the guru's kindness.

Day and night, in all six times,[1] through strong
    devotion,
I am always with the authentic guru.
I, the inseparable yogin, am happy.
This happy yogin experiences joy.
This experience of joy is the guru's kindness.

This Song of the Six Confidences
I offer to the ear of glorious Taklung Thangpa.
I don't feel that I attended the guru for a short time.
He accepted me, and taught me fully.

Notes

1. The six periods of the day.

Supplication to Tara

Jigten Sumgön had a vision of the Seven Taras at the
Echung Cave, and sang this song:

In the unborn Dharmadhatu
abides the Reverend Mother, the deity Tara.
She bestows happiness on all sentient beings.
I request her to protect me from all fears.

Through not understanding oneself as
    Dharmakaya,
one's mind is overpowered by the kleshas.
Our mothers, sentient beings, wander in samsara.
Please protect them, Deity Mother.

If the meaning of dharma is not born in one's heart,
one just follows the words [of conventional
    meaning].
Some are deceived by dogma.
Please protect them, Perfect Mother.

It is difficult to realize one's mind.
Some realize, but do not practice.
Their minds wander to worldly activities.
Please protect them, Deity Mother of Recollection.

Non-dual wisdom is the self-born mind.
By the habits of grasping at duality,
some are bound, no matter what they do.
Please protect them, Deity of Non-Dual Wisdom.

Although some abide in the perfect meaning,[1]
they don't understand the interdependence of cause
    and effect.
They are ignorant of the meaning of objects of
    knowledge.
Please protect them, Omniscient Deity Mother.

The nature of space is free from elaboration.
Nothing is different from that.
Still, practitioners and disciples [don't realize this].
Please protect them, Perfect Buddha Mother.

Notes

1. *Shunyata.*

The Song that Clarifies Recollection

Once, when Jigten Sumgön was residing at Drikung Thel, he gathered his students in a meadow behind the monastery and asked them to perform displays of their miracle power. All but one were able to comply with their guru's request, and this disciple, Rinchen Drak, suddenly died from shame. When the undertakers tried to dismember his corpse in order to feed it to the vultures, the body resisted the knife. Jigten Sumgön placed his walking stick on the heart-center of the corpse and sang this song:

I bow at the feet of glorious Phagmo Drupa.

Listen, Rinchen Drak, my son.
Ka! At the time of death ...

Worldly activities are a lie.
The eight worldly dharmas[1] are like the color of a
    rainbow.
Think, can you put your trust in them?

When you see the separation of gathered friends,
the affection of relatives and friends is a lie.[2]
Heart-felt words are like an echo.
Think, can you put your trust in them?

When you see the growth and decline of the four
    elements of the body,
the illusion of strength and ability is also a lie.
The spring flower of youth —
Think, can you put your trust in it?

When you see the gathering and consumption of
    wealth,
clinging and painful accumulation are also lies.
Food and wealth are like dew on a blade of grass.
Think, can you put your trust in them?

When you see the suffering of birth and death,
the happiness of the assemblies of gods and men is a
    lie.
The joy and suffering of the wheel of samsara —
Think, can you put your trust in them?

To the tree, the father, bodhicitta,[3]
the bias of disciples is a lie.
Nonvirtuous and misleading friends —
Think, can you put your trust in them?

When you understand that all sentient beings are
    your parents,
attachment to self-cherishing is a lie.
The Shravakas' vehicle of self-liberation —
Think, can you put your trust in it?

When you become convinced of the cause and result
    of karma,
The instruction of non-effort[4] is a lie.
Thunder without rain in an empty sky —
Think, can you put your trust in it?

For the guru who has the realization of power and
    blessings,
the obstacle of maras and error is a lie.
Chattering prayers like a parrot —
Think, can you put your trust in that?

When you realize the nature of your mind,
the three limitless kalpas are also a lie.
The deceptive vehicle of relative truth —
Think, can you put your trust in it?

In the cemetery, Gathering Relics, are you sad, son,
   at being alone?

Since nothing lasts and all must die, Rinchen Drak,
   don't be attached.

If your mind is still attached, transfer it to your
   guru's heart.

Rinchen Drak's body was then cut open and found to contain numerous relics. There were so many of these that they had to be swept together with brooms.[5]

Notes

1. Concern with gain and loss, pleasure and pain, fame and disgrace, and kind and harsh words.
2. This isn't to say that human beings don't feel genuine affection for each other, but that relationships are impermanent, and nothing to cling to as ultimately real.
3. This is a metaphor that compares bodhicitta, which is without bias, to a sheltering tree and protecting father.
4. An advanced teaching in Vajrayana that can lead to carelessness if not properly understood.
5. The cemetery where this miracle occurred was thereafter referred to as Ten Chak Gang ("Gathering Relics"). There, Jigten Sumgön opened a mandala for the purification of the lower realms, which was placed under a large slab of stone. Under that slab, he also created a light which will burn until the end of this kalpa, and which benefits the minds of those whose bodies are brought there, causing them to be free from birth in lower realms.

The Fivefold Profound Path of Mahamudra: The Practice of the Essence of Tantric Teaching

With body, speech, and mind, I prostrate and take refuge in the body, speech, and mind of the great, peerless Drikungpa[1] who is inseparable from the buddhas of the three times and unmatched in the three worlds; whose name is as famous in the ten directions as the sun and moon; the leader who liberates all sentient beings from samsara; the great lama whose limitless activities of body, speech, and mind continue without end.

The ceaseless change of all inner and outer phenomena and the great suffering of all sentient beings cause terror and fear, and sentient beings are wearied by the actions of attachment and aversion which cause them only negative karma resulting in rebirth in lower realms. There is no possibility of satisfying the needs of relatives and friends no matter how much regard we have for them. Until old age and death, one makes friends and accumulates wealth, but these are of no avail when death comes. Whoever is wise in the ways of the world attains no positive result but only deceives himself; whoever considers himself knowledgeable in the understanding and expression of intellectual things cannot separate from attachment and aversion; whoever wishes only to attain more religious teachings and outer practices will have instead further obscuration bringing the mara of pride; whoever makes great efforts to practice the precious teachings and accumulate merit in this life should make sure that the motivation comes not from attachment to this life.

If the teachings are received only from the "word" or relative lineage and not from the "meaning" or absolute lineage, then it will be like "bazaar milk" — thin and watery without the butter of suchness. Meditators who fear death and thus give up worldly activities to practice for a favorable life after death, will experience a lesser practice because of thinking about life's necessities. Even if one meditates in a solitary place, but lacks devotion and confidence, he will not actualize suchness. If one considers his *samadhi* practice sufficient but cannot relate to the things that arise in his mind and understand their interdependent nature, then he will not be able to integrate the world of appearances into his practice. If one cannot practice self-awareness, the result of one's practice will be easily dissipated by thoughts and outer conditions. If one does not receive teachings from the "blessing" or realization lineage, one cannot attain enlightenment. All ordinary words and books together will just become excess baggage.

The teaching of experience and realization from Vajradhara (Dorje Chang) is unbroken to the present time. The path of the buddhas of the three times, the practice and intentions of the Kagyudpa lamas, the heart of the Tripitaka, and the essence of the four tantras are the fivefold profound path. Even if the roof falls, the ground below breaks open, rocks crack on our left, and trees split apart on our right — it is essential to practice these five dharmas and not be distracted by the clever words of inexperienced teachers. If one practices the five dharmas and remains in the dharmata [the nature of suchness], then all faults will be transformed into virtues; all hindrances and obstacles will be transformed into attainments (siddhis); and in one lifetime one can become inseparable from the body, speech, and mind of Vajradhara.

In starting this practice, one should not have any attachment to this life — even to a single tip of one hair — and should stay in a solitary place such as a cemetery, forest, grove of trees, or empty cave. In such a place, whatever conditions of hardship or pleasure come to the body, speech, and mind, one's practice should focus on nondualistic suchness. In the Dompa Jungwa tantric text, it is said:

> The practitioner yogi should
> stay in a solitary place such
> as a cemetery and meditate with
> single-pointed mind. In such a
> place one should sit with back
> straight, not lying down or
> leaning backwards. Sit in the
> perfect lotus posture with the
> five samadhi characteristics
> of perfect position.

Bodhicitta Motivation

One's motivation is the realization that all is impermanent; that the activities and wealth of this life are like a bubble in the water; and that all sentient beings, who are limitless as the sky, have been my parents in countless lifetimes. All these sentient beings, because of delusions, sustain the ego, thus creating much negative karma through attachment, aversion, and ignorance and hence they are wandering in the six realms of samsara with no protectors and experiencing immeasurable suffering. Wearing the armor of motivation, one should perform the virtuous deeds of body, speech, and mind until death. Specifically, one must begin virtuous deeds of body, speech, and mind starting this very day, this very moment. One should engage in this practice with body, speech, and mind for the sake of all sentient beings that they might experience happiness, be separated from suffering, and attain Buddhahood. Without this kind of motivation, whatever practice one does will not lead to the perfect path. With this precious mind motivation, then all activities of body, speech, and mind will lead to the perfect path, Buddhahood.

This motivation should not be in the mind in just a relative way but should be born from one's essential being, from one's heart and in the marrow of one's bones. If someone comes to rob, kill, maim, or slander and one responds in anger acting in kind — then one is just a bodhisattva in name only. A true bodhisattva is one who wishes that all sentient beings — especially enemies who hate one, demons who hate one, and maras who cause obstacles in one's path to liberation and enlightenment — experience happiness, be separated from suffering, and attain the state of perfect completion as soon as possible. A true bodhisattva practices toward this end without selfish experience and having generated his body, wealth, and merit collected through virtue to all sentient beings.

Yidam Practice
With bodhicitta motivation one practices the yidam practice. The deities are the natural form of all sentient beings so one is not visualizing what is not — the *skandhas, dhatus,* and *ahyatanas* are the five buddhas, the five goddesses, and the bodhisattvas from beginningless time. It is said in the *Shri Sambhuti Tantra:*

> The five skandhas are the five buddhas;
> The vajra ahyatana is the mandala of the
>   bodhisattvas;
> The element of earth is Buddha Locana;
> The element of water is Mamaki;

The element of fire is Pandara — Vasini;
The element of air is Samaya-Tara.

One is a buddha from beginningless time but does not recognize it and remains in ordinary form. Thus one does not express the activities of a buddha. For example, if one cannot recognize the wish-fulfilling gem and it remains in the mud, then it will never fulfill wishes. When one receives instructions from the precious lama, one actualizes all skandhas, dhatus, and ahyatanas as the Buddha. This is the nature of Shri Heruka, the union of *yabyum*, the nondualistic wisdom body. One visualizes clearly the color, the accountrements, the ornaments, and the marks of the Buddha. By practicing this visualization with bodhicitta, one attains the ordinary and special siddhis. This yidam body blesses and transforms all outer phenomena, benefits oneself, and brings the cause of happiness to all sentient beings. Therefore one should constantly recognize this yidam and practice it. Some say the body that one visualizes in the practice now is impure and will be replaced later by a different body as a result of the practice — this falls into the dualistic confusion of doubt and hope. It is said in the *Shri Sambhuti Tantra:*

This body is Buddha —
There is no other.
One who believes Buddha is other than this body,
Is blinded by the veils of ignorance.

Guru Yoga Practice
Practicing the yidam, one visualizes the guru who is the essence of the body, speech, and mind of the buddhas of the three times and keeping one's mind inseparable from the body, speech, and mind of the guru all the obscurations and hindrances will vanish and one will attain both the relative and ultimate peace, knowledge, and happiness. It is said in the *Hevajra Tantra:*

The inexpressible coemergent wisdom

Cannot be found in the external —
It can only be found in the deeper devotion
To the guru and in one's developed virtues.

The guru who introduces one to self-awareness wisdom and thus blesses one is more kind than all the buddhas of the three times and is in essence the embodiment of all the buddhas. If one meditates on the guru at the center of one's heart and with full devotion prays constantly, then one will attain all the characteristics of the Buddha. It is said in the great *Atikoepa Tantra:*

In the tantric practice,
One who visualizes the kind guru
In the heart; in the palm of the hand;
And at the crown of the head —
Will attain the characteristics of the thousand
  buddhas.

In the *Gyutruldrawa Tantra* it is said:

Not close-by, not far away,
but always inseparable.
One should prostrate during the three times
And should place the guru
In the palace of one's heart.

If one doesn't have absolute devotion in the guru and/or sees him as an ordinary being, then any blessings one might receive will not result in the omniscient knowledge of the supermundane even though one laments, prostrates, circumambulates, and undergoes ascetic deprivation, because in the pure field of the guru one has planted the seed of wrong view. In the *Guhyasamaja Tantra* it is said:

Without oars, the ship cannot cross the ocean —
Likewise, one cannot cross samsara without the
  guru
Even though one may possess all knowledge.

One may think the buddhas of the past are gone, the

buddhas of the future have not yet come, and the buddhas of the present time have not remained with us, but there are not one, two, a hundred, or even a thousand buddhas — there are countless buddhas blessing the guru who transmits the blessings to us. That is why it is necessary to see the guru as the completely perfected Buddha Vajradhara and to pray constantly to him.

Mahamudra Meditation

Thus one keeps body, speech, and mind inseparable from the body, speech, and mind of the guru. Samsara and nirvana are conceptualizations of one's own mind. The inner truth of mind is unborn from beginningless time like the center of the sky. One should keep the mind without any positive or negative dualistic conceptions. The realization of the nature of mind, which is non-existent and unborn, is called *Mahamudra*. The great Brahmin Saraha said:

> No thought is the body of Mahamudra —
> Yogis! Do not expect any fruit or result.

There is no object within emptiness (Mahamudra) to meditate upon, nor is there any shape or color inwardly. Past, present, and future buddhas do not see the suchness of mind. In the *Guhyasamaja Tantra* it is said:

> The nature of emptiness is free from all existent
>   things —
> From skandha, dhatu, and ahyatana,
> Free from grasping and fixation.
> There is no attachment to dharma;
> Everything is equanimity and one's mind is unborn
> From beginningless time.

There is no concept, meditator, or meditation; *this* is the meditation. In the *Hevajra Tantra* it is said:

> Not meditating with the mind
> Is actually meditating.
> If one realizes dharmata —

Non-meditation is meditation.

If one has expectations or doubts in the Mahamuudra meditation then one will not cross the suffering of samsara. With effortless, mindful awareness one should meditate. To the extent that one can remain in this state, to that extent one becomes inseparable from the precious guru and non-dual with the Dharmakaya wisdom of all the buddhas. It is said in the *Phagpa Daka Yeshe Sutra:*

> If one realizes the nature of the mind,
> This is wisdom!
> One should not look for the Buddha outside the
>   mind.

One should constantly remain in the state of unborn dharmata and dedicate the merit attained for the realization of Buddhahood.

Dedication of Merit
To give benefit and bring happiness to all sentient beings, one should, without the distractions of conflicting emotions, cultivate bodhicitta along with loving kindness and compassion. To pacify the outer and inner obstacles and actualize the tantric activities, one should arise as the yidam. In order to receive the knowledge of the guru, one must have complete devotion and diligence. To progress in the practice of Mahamudra, one must remain in the state of the non-duality of tranquility meditation and activity so that the *dhyana* mind and active mind are inseparable. One should dedicate the merit attained for the total enlightenment of oneself and all sentient beings. Dedicating in this way, one attains the object of one's dedication. It is said in the *Arya Ratna Kuta Sutra:*

> As all dharmas depend on conditions,
> So the motivation becomes the goal.
> Whatever one's aspirations
> They will be achieved.

By dedicating the relative and wisdom root virtues with the two kinds of bodhicitta, these virtues will become limitless as the sky, Dharmadhatu, and numberless as the sentient beings. If one actualizes this suchness in the *Dharmakaya*, then subject, object, and action become free from all elaborations. This non-conceptual dedication is the most excellent. It is said by Maitreya in the *Abhisamaya Alamkara:*

This special way —
Sharing merit through non-conceptualization,
Without expectation —
Is the most excellent of deeds.

Transforming the Conflicting Emotions onto the Path of Enlightenment:
While remaining in non-conceptual meditation, one should realize the non-duality of the negative and positive which arise as a result of conflicting emotions and thoughts. If one does not realize the non-duality experience, then giving up conceptualization, and the attachment to the experience of no-thought will not lead to the path of enlightenment, even if one practices for kalpas. Just as waves arise in the ocean, so countless thoughts and conflicting emotions arise; just as waves are not separate from the ocean, neither are the countless thoughts and conflicting emotions separate from the unborn dharmata.

Recognition of conflicting thoughts and emotions is the Dharmakaya. Unity of the non-duality of the born and unborn is the *Sambhogakaya*. Creativity of thought is the *Nirmanakaya*. Thought without color, form, or the creativity of mind is *Svabhavakakaya*. Whatever forceful or calm thoughts or conflicting emotions arise, neglect them not but strive to see them with mindful awareness, not following but transforming them into practice. It is said in the *Chandra Prakasha Sutra:*

Whatever is born from conditions

Is unborn because it has no real birth.
Whatever depends on conditions is shunyata.
Whoever actualizes shunyata has awareness.

Meditation on the realization of Dharmakaya results in the recognition of mind as unborn form beginningless time. One should cultivate bodhicitta motivation to the end that all sentient beings, as limitless as the sky and especially those with strong attachment or aversion, may have peace and happiness; may be separated from suffering; and may quickly attain enlightenment. With this pure motivation one will arise as the yidam expressing total devotion to the guru. The arising of thoughts or conflicting emotions is one's own mind. The transforming of all thoughts and conflicting emotions is the nature of the ceaseless activities of the body, speech, and mind of the different buddha families. In the *Hevajra Tantra* it is said:

Samsara and nirvana,
These do not exist —
One who realizes the
nature of samsara
Has achieved nirvana.

One should bring all the conflicting emotions and thoughts into the relative bodhicitta. When one realizes the relative bodhicitta as the nature of four *kayas* which is free from birth, cessation, and existence — then whatever arises is the activity of the four kayas of the Buddha. Whatever thought comes, one should not look at the negative aspect. Whatever conditions arise — persons, location, behavior, emotions, and so forth — one should transform these conditions and realize their non-duality.

Transforming of Sickness onto the Path of Enlightenment
All conflicting emotions and obstacles appear from the outside. Mind and air follow in the channels of attachment, aversion, and ignorance and from this the appearances of different demons arise — male, female, and naga. Ultimate-

ly there is nothing which brings harm, and these entities which seem to bring harm have been one's mother in countless lifetimes. Those sentient beings who are suffering from negative karma cause harm, like madmen who have no control over their actions. As a result of these harmful actions, they suffer rebirth in the lower realms — wandering endlessly in the circle of samsara having no protectors or helpers. One should not oppose these beings but allow them to take whatever they desire — one's body, flesh, blood, bones, organs, intestines, speech, knowledge, intellect, or the fruits of one's meditation. One should give up any or all of these without expectation. Through the cultivation of bodhicitta one wishes that all sentient beings, especially those who cause harm, may have peace and happiness; may be separated from suffering; and may attain Buddhahood. With this enlightened attitude, one arises as the yidam with full awareness of the guru at the heart-point. The appearance of harm is just a projection of mind (Dharmakaya) which is unborn since beginningless time. There is no one who causes harm; no one who is harmed; nothing exists. The suchness of mind is free from all elaboration like the center of the sky, and in this state of non-conceptualization one will bring to clarity the non-dual nature of acceptance and rejection. In the *Gyacherolpa Sutra* it is said:

> The king of the Shakya realized
> The non-existence of all interdependent dharmas.
> His wisdom is like the sky —
> Fearing not even the delusions of a horde of maras.

[A man] may at first see a rope as a snake. After he realizes it is a rope, he then no longer sees a snake. Likewise, even though one may see demons — male, female, and naga — they are just a projection of Dharmakaya mind. Therefore one does not see the demon as something to reject, and by going to solitary places and meditating, one transforms the conception of the demon into the realization of the non-duality of acceptance and rejection.

In the same way, a yogi suffering from sickness and pain knows it is the arising of negative karma which obscures the fundamental pure awareness of the mind thus causing the conception of self and others, attachment towards positive objects, aversion towards negative objects, and indifference towards all others. From indifference the dull, unclear mind arises.

The three poisons — ignorance, attachment, and aversion — stay in the three parts of the body — upper, middle, and lower, or left, middle, and right. Through attachment we have blood and bile; through aversion we have air and catarrh; through ignorance we have phlegm. If we go to a physician he will tell us these symptoms are caused by disease and will give us medicine; if we go to a fortune-teller he will tell us they are caused by ghosts and will perform an exorcism. This is like opening and closing a window in a room to get rid of smoke instead of simply fixing the fire in the fireplace; or it is like striking out at the shadow instead of the form which casts the shadow. Although we hold this body, which is composed of the four elements, in our thoughts as a body, it does not exist. Ultimately there is no body from the beginning, so there can be no characteristics of the body such as sickness. This clarity of thought is free from being born, dying, or existing — it is pervading emptiness from the beginning. When you get sick, it is sickness of the thought. When the conception of sickness and suffering appears one should accept it fully and practice transforming the body into the stainless nectar of blessing and offering it to all sentient beings, especially those who harm us. We should cultivate bodhicitta for all sentient beings that they may be separated from suffering and attain the ultimate precious enlightenment. With this attitude, one arises as the yidam — the non-dual unity of appearance and emptiness — and meditates with utmost devotion in the guru. When we actualize our mind as Dharmakaya, free from all elaboration, unborn from the beginning — then whatever suffering we experience from sickness, to that extent the same amount of negative karmic propensities will be purified. When we see dishwater becoming cloudy from different kinds of dirt, we know the pot is being cleaned. Likewise when we actualize coemergent self-awareness as Dharmakaya wisdom, then there is no accepting or rejecting this suffering of sickness. The great Brahmin Saraha said:

> Even a kalpa of darkness
> Will be driven away in an instant by light.
> Likewise, the strong samsaric propensities
> Will be driven away in an instant by the realization
> of the true nature of one's mind.

Thus whatever sickness and suffering come, we should not depend on medicines and treatments but should earnestly practice to actualize the non-duality which is free from acceptance and rejection.

Transforming the Experience of Death

For this illusory body of the five skandhas, there will be no fear or fright at the time of death if we have done the practice and transformed the negative conditions. When one actualizes the different thoughts of the four elements, whether forceful or calm, in the non-dualistic state, there will be no intermediate state between rebirths. The experience of the habit of the dharmata is actualized in the non-dualistic state of the bardo. This is like the full moon setting and the dawn appearing without any gap of darkness between. When death comes one gives one's body, wealth, and the root of all one's virtues to the guru and the triple gem without any expectations, and cultivates bodhicitta to the end that all the numberless sentient beings who were once one's mother may possess joy; be separated from suffering; and quickly attain the precious Buddhahood. With this attitude, one arises as the yidam, the unity of appearance and emptiness. One foot above the crown of one's head (the Brahma door) one visualizes a lion throne upon which rests a many-petalled lotus, and a sun and moon disc seat upon which sits one's own precious root-guru who is the embodiment of all the buddhas of the three times. One's consciousness in the form of the red letter HUNG is at the navel point rising up the transparent central channel through the crown of the head, dissolving into the guru's heart and becoming inseparable from the guru's wisdom-body (*Jnanakaya*). One should meditate in this state of the inseparability of one's mind and the guru. Thus Shantideva said in the *Bodhicharyavatara:*

> As through alchemy, iron transmutes into gold —
> Likewise, this filthy body transforms into the
>   priceless precious buddha-body
> Through the power of bodhicitta.
> Hold this attitude firmly in the mind.

In this way, the veils of the four defilements are eliminated and one attains the state of the fully enlightened Vajradhara, the perfect Buddhahood inseparable from the three kayas *(Trikaya)*. It is said in the *Naljorma Kuntu-Cho Tantra:*

> A yogi who transfers his consciousness —
> by Shri Heruka and others who hold flowers in their
>   hands;
> Hold different victorious banners;
> And make different musical sounds —
> By them, this yogi will be received in the
>   buddhafield when the thought called death
>   arises.

Thus, following the direction of a qualified guru, one who realizes this mind which is unborn from the beginning can realize the Dharmakaya which is pure from the beginning. By one's own efforts and practice one realizes the non-duality free from acceptance or rejection. In this way one can achieve the highest buddhafield and attain enlightenment. Thus it is said in the *Khadroma Dorje Gur:*

> Oh, the highest attainment is Buddha.

One can attain Buddhahood by practicing mind.
Outside of this precious mind
There are no buddhas or sentient beings.

From this Dharmakaya, activities of body, speech, and mind benefit all sentient beings appropriately until the end of samsara, like a wish-fulfilling gem. These activities of body, speech, and consciousness are beyond conception and limitless like the revolutions of a continuously turning wheel. It is said in the *Palgongpa Lungton Tantra:*

Beyond conception, like the sky —
The bodhi-mind vajraholder,
Tathagata comes for all sentient beings
Like the wish-fulfilling gem.

Thus, if one practices this complete path, not missing any of these five practices — one can purify all imperfections, cause to arise all knowledge, and attain the highest buddha-field. The essence of the *Tripitakas* and the four tantras of Buddha's teaching is this fivefold profound path which includes all techniques and teachings. If one of the practices is missing, the result will not include the fruit. To emphasize again how important this practice is, one should not follow second or third-hand incomplete teaching. Once one finds the elephant, one does not need to search for the footprints. Practice this fivefold profound path continuously in a solitary place with complete diligence and devotion.

This nectar teaching essence of heart is from the great Drikungpa Lord Jigten Sumgön, the unequalled one, and is composed by the bhikshu Shila Ratna of Buddha Shakyamuni.

Ach'i Chökyi Drölma

Ach'i Chökyi Drölma is the great dharma protector of the Buddha's teachings. She is the emanation of Vajrayogini who is the embodiment of the wisdom and activities of all the buddhas. She is the divine mother of the buddhas and manifested out of compassion in the form of the dakinis of the five buddha families. To benefit the beings in samsara, she displays a limitless number of manifestations at different times and in different space dimensions.

✶   ✶   ✶

In the country of Uddiyana where Vajrayana originated is the divine palace where Vajrayogini manifested in the form of Vajra-Dakini and made the commitment to protect the Buddha's teachings. This commitment she made to the five families of wisdom-dakinis.

Later in the eighth century when Guru Padmasambhava was invited to Tibet to spread the dharma teachings, he blessed many places in Tibet and meditated in many caves. Among these caves was Ti-dro, a cave in the area of Drikung, where Guru Padmasambhava spent seven years. This is the longest time he spent in any one place in Tibet.

During this period Vajrayogini manifested in the form of the chief karma-dakini and promised to protect the Vajrayana teachings.

These are manifestations in Jnanakaya (wisdom-body)
through which she benefited the precious teachings and all
sentient beings. According to prophecy in the *Chakrasamvara Tantra*, it is
said that the head of the karma-dakinis will come to the area
of Ti-dro cave in Drikung. This will be a Nirmanakaya[1]
manifestation of Vajrayogini.

Around the eleventh century in Shotoe, in the area of
Drikung in Central Tibet, there lived a family who could
not conceive a child. In order to bear a child they made a
pilgrimage to Swayambhu in Nepal. They prayed fervently
for a child and one night the woman, Driza Darzam, had a
dream that a brightly shining sun appeared in the east and
radiated light in the ten directions and the sun then dissolved into her womb and radiated light which filled the
whole universe, especially illuminating the country of her
birth. In the same night her husband, Nanam Chowopal,
had a dream that a rosary of clear white light emanated from
the eastern buddha-field and entered the womb of his wife.
In the morning they discussed their dreams and he said, "A
special son will be born to us and we should take much care
until this child is born." They performed a *tsog* offering,
made strong prayer to fulfil their wishes, and then returned
to their native land in Drikung.

The time came for the birth and an extraordinary daughter was born in the place called Kyetrag Thang. There were
numerous auspicious signs, and her body was of purest
white and radiating rays of light. As a small child she was
always reciting the mantra of Tara and at the age of three
she was teaching the mantra to others. She grew quickly
and was incredibly beautiful. Her parents died when she
was quite young and she then stayed with her uncle. Many
wanted to marry her but she refused all, stating, "I will go to
Kham in Eastern Tibet where there lives a great yogi who is
descended from the noble clan of the Kyura race. This yogi
I will marry, and our sons and grandsons and the future
generations will be extraordinary individuals who will be-

nefit all sentient beings by spreading the essence of the Buddha's teachings." Then, accompanying a merchant, she traveled to Kham. They arrived at a place called Dentod Tso-ngur and she said to her companion, "This is the place I have to stay." She departed and went to meet the great saint, Ame Tsültrim Gyatso, to whom she said, "Although I have no attachment to the worldly life, if we join together our descendants will bear many enlightened beings who will do great benefit for the teachings of the Buddha." On their marriage day, Ame Tsültrim Gyatso did not have any possessions to arrange for the ceremony. Drölma said, "Do not worry, I will take care of it." So saying she miraculously pulled a *damaru* (drum) from her right pocket and a *kapala* (skull-cup) from her left. Then beating the damaru and holding the kapala in her hand she made a mystic dance while gazing into the sky. Immediately the house was filled with the finest food and drink and the richest garments with which to clothe themselves — thus giving great satisfaction and pleasure to all the guests.

They lived together and in time she gave birth to four sons: Namkhe Wangchuk, Pekar Wangyal, Sönam Pal, and Kathung Trushi. These sons were exceptionally intelligent and became great learned scholars on both the temporal and spiritual levels.

At a later time, Drölma said, "I have knowingly taken birth into samsara in order to fulfil my aspirations to protect the teachings of the Buddha and for the welfare of all sentient beings. Because of this, I will grant the ordinary and the supreme siddhis to my followers." She led her followers to a huge cave called Ting-ring. The cave was very sacred, containing many precious termas (hidden treasures) and many self-created statues of the buddhas, bodhisattvas, yidams, dakinis, and dharma protectors on the rocks inside the cave. A human corpse was brought and she transformed that corpse into a great tsog offering. Those who could partake of that tsog were granted the ordinary and the supreme siddhis. Then she composed a text containing a sadhana of herself and promised to look after the teachings of the Buddha in general and to protect the great essence of the Buddha's teaching that will appear in the future. With that she said, "My activities through this body have come to an end" and she flew up to the buddha-field on her blue horse without leaving her body. Of her four sons, Pekar Wangyal fathered four sons. They were: Khenpo Darma, Könchok Rinchen, Tsünpa Bar, and Naljor Dorje — of these four, Naljor Dorje became the father of the great Ratna-shri Jigten Sumgön, the great Drikungpa who was the reincarnation of Nagarjuna. Once when Jigten Sumgön was staying at Changchubling in Drikung-thel, the sound of a damaru accompanied by beautiful celestial songs was heard. Drub-thob Khambagyagarwa, a great yogi disciple, was there and asked Jigten Sumgön about the beautiful music. Jigten Sumgön said: "The incomparable sounds are from Ach'i[2] Chökyi Drölma, my grandmother, who is a wisdom-dakini."

Then Drub-thob Khamba insistently requested that he be given a method on how to practice Ach'i Chökyi Drölma and thus Jigten Sumgön composed a sadhana consisting of ten leaves which is contained in the *Ach'i Pe-bum.*

In the *Me-che Barwa Tantra* Buddha says: "After limitless kalpas in a world system called Pema-chan, she will become the perfectly enlightened Bhagavan, Tathagata, Arhat, Samyak Sambuddha — whose name will be Pema Dampe-pal."

This is the life of the great Ach'i Chökyi Drölma, the peerless compassionate dharma protector who committed herself to the service of the buddhadharma and benefited all sentient beings. She promised Jigten Sumgön Ratna-shri, the great Drikungpa, to protect the essence of the Buddha's teaching which he brought to light and transmitted through the lineage of the Drikung Kagyudpa order. Because of this promise, whosoever will practice the sadhana of Ach'i Chökyi Drölma with full devotion and certainty will be freed from all kinds of unfavourable circumstances and obstacles in this life and also obstacles connected with dharma practice. Those who continue doing the practice with full faith and devotion will finally achieve the perfectly enlightened state, Buddhahood.

This abbreviated history is based on text composed by His Holiness Drikung Kyabgön Chetsang Rinpoche — translated and printed on the occasion of the opening of the Drikung Kagyudpa Tibetan Meditation Center in Washington, D.C. in October, 1983.

Ruling over the three realms of existence and
   protecting all beings without exception;
Protecting the teachings of the thousand buddhas of
   this fortunate kalpa;
And fulfilling the wishes of all sentient beings
   according to their desire —
Through your power to fulfil our wishes, Ach'i
   Chökyi Drölma please bestow the glory of your
   blessings now.

Notes

1. Nirmanakaya is the form-body manifestation through which an enlightened being helps all sentient beings.
2 .*Ach'i* means grandmother.

Glossary

ACHARYA — A learned teacher.
ARHAT — One who has overcome conflicting emotions.
AVADHUTI — The central channel of the body.
AVALOKITESHVARA — A deity, the embodiment of the compassion of all buddhas.
BARDO — The intermediate state between death and rebirth.
BHUMI — Level of a bodhisattva's attainment.
BODHI — Enlightenment, full purification of mental obscurations and completion of wisdom.
BODHICITTA — Enlightened attitude.
BODHISATTVA — One who has the enlightened attitude.
BUDDHA — A fully-enlightened being.
CHAKRASAMVARA — A yidam.
CHAKRAVARTIN — A universal monarch.
CHANG — Tibetan beer.
DAKA — Male embodiment of tantric energy.
DAKINI — Female embodiment of tantric energy.
DHARMA — The Buddha's teachings, what is taught and what is realized through practice; also, anything which can be known by mind.
DHARMACHAKRA — The Wheel of Dharma.
DHARMADHATU — The true nature of all dharma.
DHARMAKAYA — The form of dharma.
DHARMATA — "Thatness," the nature of reality.

GARUDA — A special bird possessing great power.

GESHE — Spiritual friend.

GUHYASAMAJA — A yidam.

GURU — Teacher.

INTERDEPENDENT ORIGINATION — *Pratitya samutpada.*

JAMBUDVIPA — The southern continent, according to the Buddhist world-system.

KALPA — Eon.

KARMA — Cause and effect.

KAYAS — Forms of a buddha.

KLESHAS — Conflicting emotions.

MAHAMUDRA — The Great Seal, the ultimate view of the Buddha's teachings.

MAHAPANDITA — A great scholar.

MAHASIDDHA — One with great realization.

MAHAYANA — The Greater Vehicle, which concerns itself with the saving of all sentient beings from suffering.

MAITREYA — The coming fifth buddha.

MANDALA — A grouping of certain principles into a circle.

MANJUSHRI — A deity, the embodiment of the wisdom of all buddhas.

MANTRA — That which protects the mind, usually a phrase or a name associated with deities or buddhas that is repeated to oneself.

MARAS — Obstacle-causing demons.

NAGA — A serpent-being.

NIRVANA — The cessation of suffering.

ODDIYANA — The name of a buddha-field.

PARINIRVANA — The death of an enlightened being.

PRANA — Inner wind.

SAMADHI — Meditative absorption.

SAMSARA — The cycle of rebirth in conditions of suffering.

SANGHA — Those intent on liberation.

SHRAVAKA — One who hears and proclaims the dharma.

SHUNYATA — All-pervading openness.

SIDDHI — Attainment.

STUPA — A special receptacle for offerings.

SUGATA — A name of the Buddha.

SUTRA — Those teachings of the Buddha which do not require empowerment to study and practice.

TANTRA — Those teachings which do require empowerment to study and practice.

TANTRIKA — A practitioner of tantra.

TARA — A female deity, the embodiment of the activity of all buddhas.

TATHAGATA — A name of the Buddha.

TERMA — Hidden treasure: teachings, images, or wealth.

TORMA — Offering-cakes.

UPASAKA — A lay follower of the Buddha who holds the five precepts: not to kill, not to steal, not to engage in sexual misconduct, not to lie, and not to drink alcohol.

VAJRA — Thunderbolt scepter, symbolizing indestructibility.

VAJRADHARA — The Primordial Buddha.

VAJRAYANA — The Indestructible Vehicle.

VAJRAYOGINI — A semi-wrathful female yidam.

VIDYADHARA — One who holds awareness-wisdom.

VINAYA — The rules of monastic discipline.

YAMANTAKA — a wrathful yidam.

YIDAM — One's personal deity.

YOGIN — One who has realized the nature of reality.